ROUTLEDGE LIBRARY EDITIONS:
COMMUNICATION STUDIES

Volume 2

UNDERSTANDING COMMUNICATION

UNDERSTANDING COMMUNICATION

The Signifying Web

D. J. CROWLEY

Routledge
Taylor & Francis Group
LONDON AND NEW YORK

First published in 1982 by Gordon and Breach, Science Publishers, Inc.

This edition first published in 2016
by Routledge
2 Park Square, Milton Park, Abingdon, Oxon OX14 4RN

and by Routledge
711 Third Avenue, New York, NY 10017

Routledge is an imprint of the Taylor & Francis Group, an informa business

British Library Cataloguing in Publication Data
A catalogue record for this book is available from the British Library

ISBN: 978-1-138-93903-5 (Set)
ISBN: 978-1-315-67052-2 (Set) (ebk)
ISBN: 978-1-138-94155-7 (Volume 2) (hbk)
ISBN: 978-1-138-95944-6 (Volume 2) (pbk)
ISBN: 978-1-315-67050-8 (Volume 2) (ebk)

UNDERSTANDING COMMUNICATION
The Signifying Web

D. J. Crowley

GORDON AND BREACH SCIENCE PUBLISHERS
New York London Paris

Gordon and Breach, Science Publishers, Inc.
One Park Avenue
New York NY10016

Gordon and Breach Science Publishers Ltd.
42 William IV Street
London WC2N 4DE

Gordon & Breach
58, rue Lhomond
75005 Paris

Library of Congress Cataloging in Publication Data

Crowley, David J., 1945-
Understanding communication.

(Communication and the human condition ; v. 2)
Bibliography: p.
Includes index.
1. Communication. I. Title. II. Series.
P90.C78 001.51 82-1061
ISBN 0-677-05920-5 AACR2

ISBN 0 677 05920 5. ISSN 0275-2069.
Printed in the United States of America.

For my parents
John and Margaret Crowley

Contents

Introduction to the Series

It would be impossible to overstate the role of communication in the human condition, and in the evolution of human civilization. In communication, we construct and navigate our everyday lives. The limits of our communicable world are the limits of our lives. In our communication with one another we mediate, on the one hand, the form and the substance of our consciousness, on the other, the form and the significance of all of our social arrangements and social institutions. We create ourselves, and re-create the social/cultural milicu in which we will have our lives, in communication. Just as our histories are a matter of what we have said of them, our futures are a matter of what we may say of them.

Every human culture, every human society, every human encounter, every human being, must be *realized* in communication. What we refer to when we refer to "human nature" is nowhere to be found in nature. It is what people have made of themselves, in various cultures, at different times and in different ways, in and through communication.

All human affairs, from the everyday to the epochal, are engendered in communication. The form and the substance – the very meaning – of our lives, is given in what we can say that others will understand, and what others will understand of what we may say. What we know and how we know it, perhaps even what we can know, is given in the ways in which we do and do not communicate. Everything people do, and everything people do not do, has its motive and its motif in communication. Whatever is not *created* in communication, if it is to be part of our human lives, must be given sensibility or legitimacy *in* communication, Every feeling, every belief, every thought we may have is mediated by communication.

As we communicate, so shall we be.

Civilizations are made of words. Every human artifact – a bridge no less than a book, a political strategy no less than a mind, a sculpture no less than a world view – has its possibility and its destiny in what can be, what is, said about it. That of which we cannot speak does not exist for us. What we may speak of exists for us only in those ways in which we do speak of it. The only world we know is given to us in communication.

To be human is to be in communication. In an exceedingly eloquent and poignant passage about her early life, Helen Keller told us that to be humanly conscious requires communicability. Communicative competence is not just another useful skill, like shoemaking; it is one's ticket of admission to human and social life.

Every human entanglement – war no less than peace, hate no less than love, despair no less than hope, aggression no less than mutual cooperation, innovation no less than conservation, whether in science or politics or art or economics or everyday life – is conceived and has its life in communication. Our long-term human interests are given, or taken away, in communication. It may be that what we need in the short run is more food to feed the world's starving millions. But what we need in the long run is a way of talking about such matters that would radically alter either our ways of producing and consuming food, or our ways of producing and consuming people.

Undergirding the greatest human achievements, and the greatest human catastrophes, there has always been a compelling human belief. And human beliefs are made of words. What is, no less than what ought to be, is given in how we can, how we do, communicate.

In constructing and maintaining all that of which we may be mindful in communication, we construct and maintain ourselves. The awesome extent to which we do participate – in communication – in the creation of the conditions of our humanity, of our social and cultural lives, of our problems and possibilities, is perhaps what makes it so difficult for us to come to grips with the idea of human communication.

Whether it is the sheer difficulty of doing so, or our fear of doing so, that has impeded our understanding and appreciation of the role of communication in human life and human civilizations, there can be little excuse for the way in which twentieth-century Western thought has trivialized the idea of communication. To understand communication in any ultimate sense would surely be the crowning achievement of the human intellect: How shall we understand that process by which we understand? Yet what would we know if we knew that? And suppose we could not measure up to that knowledge? But to trivialize the idea of communication in order to make it amendable to our technicist-scientistic ways of knowing – all in the name of "science" – not only does mankind a disservice; it does science a disservice. The central issues in communication are not those that our often petty and short-sighted concerns of the day rather too easily suggest to us. The central issues are not, in fact, merely "theoretical" or merely "scientific"; they are not, in fact, issues that require only our understanding or explanation; they are, in fact, ultimately *moral* issues.

For what is at stake is no less than what, and how, we shall be.

The evolution of a human civilization is a playing out of the possibilities implicit in the ways in which a people do and do not talk about things. The human condition, whether in a family or a society, is given in that complex fabric of mental and emotional artifacts which are produced in the process of communication. *How* we do and do not communicate makes a difference. And the difference it makes is a moral one: As we communicate, so shall we be.

If anything, our grasp of the central issues involved in the idea of communication has diminished in the twentieth century. Augustine came closer to those central issues than any modern-day philosopher has. Our zealous pursuit of scientism in our understanding of everything has driven us off the mark.

What we have seen in the twentieth century is a remarkable proliferation of so-called "communication technologies". But satellites and computers and television broadcast stations and high-efficiency, high-capacity telephone circuits are not, strictly speaking, of course, "communication" technologies. They are data-transport or data-processing technologies. Yet we sometimes speak as if such gadgets as a "hot-line" or an 80,000 wpm word-processor were solving our *communication* problems. They are not. In many instances, they are exacerbating those problems.

We'd like to believe that what seems to us to be technological "progress" is a reasonable substitute for moral progress. It is not.

Knowing what one should be is not a linear function of the amount of "information" that one can command. If it were, we would certainly have entered the "Golden Age."

Ancient Chinese philosophers taught that if one "knew" something which had neither personally practical use (e.g., how to lay bricks for one's house) nor a spiritual use (i.e., in perfecting one's self as a human being), then that "knowledge" constituted an aspect of evil in the world. Perhaps they were on to something important: the more information we have, the less capable we seem to be of solving our social and political problems.

The lure of our technologies is the lure of the Sirens. We have forgotten where it was we wanted to go.

And yet . . . there is undoubtedly more intellectual interest in many of the non-trivial aspects of communication than ever before in our history. New insights, new possibilities, are being generated at the fringes of many new – and some old – areas of inquiry: semiotics, psycho- and socio-linguistics, cultural analysis, symbolic interactionism, cybernetics, ethnography, network analysis, cognitive psychology, grammatology, cultural anthropology, ethology, sociobiology, structuralism and its derivatives, discourse analysis, sociology of knowledge, praxiology, the "new" rhetoric, hermencutics, etc., etc. It is a time of ferment, of excitement, of possibility.

What is going on of importance to the study of communication is represented only in small part by the output of the academic discipline of "Communication" itself. Critical work on the idea of communication is widely dispersed, fragmented. Those coming at certain basic issues of communication from one perspective often are not even aware of what those at work from other perspectives are doing.

That the substance of this inquiry into the idea of communication is so fragmented and hodge-podge is the consequence of a complex of political machinations and historical accidents both within and without the academy. But there is no mechanism by which to redress those happenings, that condition, and put the "field" back together as if it had merely suffered a great fall, like Humpty-Dumpty.

Still, the time is ripe to undertake the publication of a series of books and monographs which might accurately and provocatively represent the scope and depth of the best work that is being done on the idea of communication today, whatever the disciplinary source or the direction of that work. Perhaps this series of books may even stimulate some ecumenism in the field. In the long run, there could hardly be an intellectual endeavor of greater potential import for the future of our civilization.

That is the rationale, and the premise, for this series.

LEE THAYER

Introduction

More than a decade ago a communication scholar observed that "our tendency to cling to untenable assumptions and our 'mythology' of communication have served as significant barriers to conceptual-theoretical progress." Since then much has happened. European scholarship, finally recovering much of its prewar vitality and intent upon rethinking its own "mythologies" of communication, once again began to make itself felt as an intellectual force. The Third World provided a different contrast. After decades of experience with development recipes, many involving communication technology, some of the most sensitive – and scathing – reappraisals of the "assumptions" about the role of communication in modernization found their way back to the developed world. Deliberately little by little, North Americans, long the doers in communication, responded to this cross-migration of intellectual and practical issues with initiatives of their own. Constructivist theory took hold, the dormant tradition of American semiotics reappeared, and the theme of culture came back into fashion. New technologies brought about policy debates that pushed communication far beyond the world of researchers and technicians into the arena of human rights and global political economy. In less than a decade communication had become an issue of substance and an object of political struggle, and surrounded by a contentious climate of opinion.

Several things should be said about how this book is written and how these themes are organized within it. First, this is a book of concepts. All forms of human understanding depend upon concepts, acknowledged or not. Clarifying conceptual issues generally presents us with two possibilities: we can approach the clarification of concepts as an intellectual task, in terms of the issues facing the human condition, and as a practical task, in terms of current social problems, operational decisions, and the questions presently facing researchers. This book attempts to relate these two tasks to one another. In reality, their separateness is another sort of "myth." In a world able to sense in concrete ways the implications of a global infrastructure of communication technologies capable of linking together immensely different regions, peoples, and forms of experience, what we call practical issues blend at many points into issues of the human condition itself.

Second, this is a book about communication – the conventions, institutions, and human practices that make up the signifying web of meanings in which we live. The issues of communication, both intellectual and practical, are far too important today to remain limited to one group of scholars or researchers, or restricted to one department of government or to one sector of the economy. Communication, after all, is a human production, and men and women are, in part, its social product.

Thirdly, this book places significant stress upon the interactional unit of analysis. It therefore departs from all those studies of communication that base themselves upon some notion of the individual as the passive receiver of communication; and especially from those studies which see both meaning and behavior arising from the direct action of messages upon individuals (the so-called manipulation thesis). With these special limitations it is possible to call the perspective offered an interactional one. Perspective is, I believe, the proper term because the argument that follows is more than mindful of the tensions between the construction of any conceptual-theoretical schematic and the pragmatic human realities it attempts to understand.

What follows then is not a synthesis of communication theories, but a rethinking and a reappraisal from one of these perspectives, through which the reader can find his or her way more deeply into the abiding themes and issues. Of course, making interpretations of this sort is also a way of providing designs and proposing alternatives – and acting thereby *for* communication.

A note on reading: the first part (Chapters 1-4) introduces some basic principles of communication (feedback and reflexion, for example) and some basic ways of classifying communication (modes, for instance). The remaining chapters are clustered around major themes and issues and arranged in such a way that the materials of the later chapters can benefit from the discussions of the earlier ones.

PART ONE

The Foundations — Feedback and Reflexion

1. The Idea of Feedback
2. Interdependency and Human Needs
3. Reflexion and the Social Order
4. Modes of Human Communication

PART ONE

"There are," the psychologist Paul Watzlawick says, "many different versions of reality, some of which are contradictory, but all of which are the results of communication and not reflections of eternal objective truths."[1]

Therapists like Watzlawick commonly deal with people who are trying to sort out and come to terms with "troubled" versions of reality. Yet, the act of sorting out and coming to terms with reality (sometimes including therapy) is part of a continuous daily process, full of struggle and conflict, at every level of human existence. In the chapters to follow this process of working out and coming to terms with reality through communication is introduced by way of the concepts of feedback and reflexion.

CHAPTER 1

The Idea of Feedback

1.1 Nature, Machines, and Culture

In 1856, while recovering from malaria in the rain forests of Indonesia, Alfred Russel Wallace wrote to Charles Darwin, then at work on *Origin of the Species*, about his own inelegant analogy for explaining natural selection. The principle of natural selection, he wrote, "is exactly like that of the centrifugal governor of the steam engine, which checks and corrects any irregularities almost before they become evident; and in like manner no unbalanced deficiency in the animal kingdom can ever reach any conspicuous magnitude because it would make itself felt at the very first step, by rendering existence difficult and extinction almost sure to follow." Darwin was no doubt quick to grasp the significance of Wallace's analogy, but so cunning in his portrayal of man as risen from monkeys and savages that it has been largely overlooked how the proposition of natural selection may have been developed by analogy with those rotating governors perched atop the steam engines of the British industrial midlands.[1]

It was, of course, the self-regulating feature of James Watt's steam engine that attracted Wallace's attention – that precise capacity of the governor to automatically adjust fuel to the work requirements of the machine so that the turning output always remains within the desired limits; and without the need for constant human monitoring. There must be in nature, Wallace speculated, a stabilizing process something like that of these machines, a way in which nature manages to keep evolutionary changes within tolerable limits. But, apart from a few items of correspondence there is little evidence to tell us whether Darwin ever seriously entertained Wallace's idea. In fact, the link between the stabilizing process in nature and the function of the governor in some machines remained little more than an unusual analogy until almost a century later when a New England mathematician, Norbert Wiener, suggested how machines and nature both depend upon forms of information processing to monitor and stabilize their activities. Wiener's work, called *cybernetics* – the science of communication and control in animals and machines – represented the first partly successful effort to fit the role of communication into the framework of nature and society.

1.2 Feedback

1.2.1 Steering – Wiener

There was, Wiener found, a principle of conservation at work in nature, in some technologies, and in all cultures by which they could allow dynamic activity yet remain within stable limits.[2] The human body, for example, must be highly efficient in maintaining a steady temperature. Sweating and shivering are normal and acceptable responses to changes in our environment, but fevers and chills are more drastic responses and, if unchecked, damaging, even fatal, to the organism. For centuries, in fact from ancient times, it had been known that the human body maintained a steady heat level through an internal process of adjustments to changes in the outer environment. By the nineteenth century this process had been identified with the function of the hypothalmic gland and labelled *homeostasis*. When the environment around it cools, the human body expends energy to raise its temperature; and when the temperature rises too high the body corrects itself through a variety of responses for cooling down. The result is homeostasis, not a steady temperature state but a perpetual oscillation, a sort of tightly controlled zig-zag pattern through an ideal setting (98.6 Fahrenheit, 37.2 Centigrade) by which an approximation of stability is maintained.

Less dramatic than the regulation of body temperature is the process by which men and women themselves act as governors to direct the performance of machines through changing environmental conditions. The internal combustion engine, for example, pushes car and driver along a highway at a constant speed barring changes in the outer environment such as hills, wind shifts, or other vehicles. Under such conditions car and driver may continue at a constant speed and with a constant use of fuel. Should the car encounter a hill, however, the load factor will immediately increase, the car slows and the driver, to recover the previous speed, will have to feed the engine more fuel until the previous speed is regained. This process of maintaining a steady relationship between an entity and its environment, whether guided by a mechanical governor, the hypothalmus, or the complex interplay of car, driver, and road conditions demonstrates the function of *information feedback*. Wiener defined feedback as the method of controlling a system by reinserting into it the results of its past performance.

Feedback is information from a changing environment; the concept of feedback helps us to see the process by which organisms and machines continuously engage in self-corrective moves through reacting to what actually happens and achieving thereby a sort of ongoing stability. It was on the basis of his description of how information feeds back from environment to the organism or the machine that Wiener was able to make his surprising claim that nature, some machines, and by implication man and his social world are stabilized through an aspect of their communication.

It is worth noting Wiener's distinction between *actual* and *intended* performance. An *intended* action may be completed much as a stone may be thrown, without reference to an outside environment; but it will not be possible to determine whether the results attained were the same as the results intended – the broken window, for instance – unless a check is made with the *actual* state of affairs in the environment. This is why elevator doors do not open when the elevator's drive system says the elevator should be at the twentieth floor, but only when the sensors on the twentieth floor indicate that it actually has arrived. Regrettably, people who walk into open elevator shafts are acting on the basis of an anticipated rather than an actual state of affairs.[3]

1.2.2 The Efficiency of Feedback – Deutsch

In activities controlled by feedback, efficiency depends upon minimizing mistakes, either the number or the extent or both. Consider the human pastime of shooting clay pigeons. The point of the sport is to hit the clay pigeon before it hits the ground. The rate of speed and the angle at which the clay pigeon flies can be controlled at launch; and for the experienced shot both the speed and the trajectory can be generally anticipated. Information is taken in visually by the shooter and coordinated into commands for aiming and firing. A clay pigeon moves rapidly so the shooter in following its flight must compensate for his own stationary position and for the lapsed time of his own responses by sighting the gun slightly ahead of the projectile. And since both the bullet and the clay pigeon travel at quite different speeds, this lead must be further calibrated to allow their paths to intersect at a projected point of impact.

The efficient reaching of any goal, like the shooting of clay pigeons, depends upon controlling mistakes. Karl Deutsch found that diminishing these mistakes depends in turn upon four factors:[4]

1. LOAD – the extent and speed of change in the position of the goal desired
2. LAG – the response time between reception of information and execution
3. GAIN – the amount of actual change from the corrective steps
4. LEAD – the distance of the predicted position from the position actually perceived

The factors of load, lag, gain, and lead all affect the outcome. Even for the skilled shooter, reducing mistakes depends upon the rapid and accurate calculation of all four factors. Design engineers have long recognized the limitations of training programs and the extent to which highly skilled tasks can be mastered. Increasingly today our technologies assign more and more of such calculation to computers, whether those of military weaponry or those of organized work. It is also why hunters, when faced with the crafty fowl instead of clay pigeons, still prefer birdshot to bullets.

1.3 Perception

1.3.1 The Ames Experiments

Adelbert Ames, Jr., was a New York ophthalmologist who worried his colleagues by his ceaseless efforts to create in normal people the sorts of perceptual distortion most specialists did their best to correct in their patients. Ames' experiments were really demonstrations meant to show how seeing is based not on direct sensations of the world around us but on something like perceptual assumptions resulting from the sorts of experience we all universally share. In retrospect, the demonstrations are rich evidence for how feedback functions in perception to stabilize our visual relation to the world about us.

1.3.2 The Rotating Trapezoidal Window

In one of Ames' demonstrations a trapezoidally shaped window is rotated slowly, at a speed where it is perceived as a rectangle, gently oscillating from side to side.[5] When a straight rod is placed in the window it appears to fold around it; a box, when placed in one corner of the window, seems to sail off into space. As Ames explained the illusion, our past experience has made us familiar with a variety of rectangular forms – doors, windows, cupboards, books. Yet, for the most part the images formed on our eye's retina by these objects is not rectangular, but trapezoidal. This is because we seldom approach rectangular forms in a direct frontal way, but rather encounter them at angles for which our vision must make some correction. Thus the trapezoidal form that appears in the retina is translated into a rectangular object seen in perspective. Through interpretation one compensates for degrees of trapezoidal distortion by adjusting the relation between the position of the form and the position of the viewpoint. Learning to act with regard to rectangular forms in perspective is what Ames meant by a commonly shared or nearly universal experience.

The Zulu people are an exception. The Zulu of the Bantu culture have less experience with man-made rectangles than the rest of us. They live in round huts, arranged in circular forms, have round stockades for animals, and cultivate fields that conform to the contours of the land. As if to complete the circle, they eat from round bowls, use rounded utensils, enter and exit through oval-shaped doors and have neither windows nor words for windows. Thus, when two Americans, Allport and Pettigrew, went to southern Africa and showed them the trapezoidal window trick, the indulgent Zulu did not see the illusion as frequently as people elsewhere. Different cultures create differences in cumulative experiences which, Allport and Pettigrew conclude, can create subtle differences in the way reality is perceived.[6] It may also be a case of the exception proving the rule; hence Ames' use of the phrase "commonly shared or nearly universal experience."

1.3.3 The Trapezoidal Room

The anthropologist Gregory Bateson was invited to look into one of Ames's trapezoidal rooms. First Bateson studied the room from above, constructed as it was to dollhouse size, and noted the rakish angles and distortions which Ames had included in the interior design. Then Bateson looked through a peephole at one end of the room with the help of a pair of prismatic glasses which distorted his binocular vision. The room appeared perfectly normal. Ames asked Bateson to touch a pointer to a sheet of paper fastened on one wall and, when he had done that successfully, to move the pointer to another piece of paper on a seemingly opposite wall. Bateson tried and tried, helplessly thumping the pointer each time into the wall at a point far from the paper. Others, Ames noted ruefully, sometimes learned to adjust for this distortion of visual experience and improve their aims accordingly, but the famous anthropologist never did. The difficulty of changing the settings of our perception, even in the case of easily acknowledged distortions, can be very difficult.

1.3.4 The Honi Phenomenon

Ames finally got a little of his own back when he asked a newly-wed couple to participate in another one of his experiments. He had constructed a monocular distorted room which appeared normal when viewed with one eye. Since the room was in fact distorted, a familiar face when seen through a window in the room would appear expanded or contracted. Alas, when Ames asked the husband to appear in the window while his new wife looked into the room from the other side, she reportedly saw only the perfect face of her handsome and loving man.[7]

When what we encounter fails to confirm our commonly held assumptions about how things are, we can have trouble accepting such a state of affairs. Or, we can fail to see these new facts at all. The importance of feedback control in maintaining a stable relationship between our perceptions and our experience seems partly confirmed by the efforts of Adelbert Ames to undermine our confidence in this process. Our perceptual assumptions, it seems, develop out of our cumulative and common experiences which, in turn, become the basis for our shared frames of reference on a reality that otherwise seems to be so convincingly "given" and "out there." In this intertwining of commonly shared experiences and perception it is the role of feedback to continuously re-assure us about the status of our perceptual assumptions.

1.4 Interaction

1.4.1 Amplifying and Goal-Changing Feedback

In addition to the feedback functions discussed so far – which is known technically as self-corrective or negative feedback – there are thought to be two other types. It is sometimes forgotten that the stabilizing function of feedback depends upon set-limits or goals being built into the relationship with the environment in some prearranged way. In the absence of such goals or limits – for instance, in the absence of a thermostat set to 20 degrees centigrade or the engine throttled to a given speed – the system in question may simply proceed until it breaks down or until it encounters other defining limits. Uncontrolled, engines and furnaces break down at high levels of activity; and both will cease to function completely when the fuel runs out. Likewise, forest fires will continue to consume all that there is to burn. And since the availability of fuel represents the limits of the fire, it is common practice for fire fighters to fight fire with fire, starting controllable counterburns to deprive the larger blaze of its fuel. This sequence of events, where the relationship between fire and fuel is not subject to regulation, but becomes in fact an escalating sequence of events, is a case of *amplifying feedback,* where more of one thing leads to more of another. Amplifying feedback, as the example of forest fires demonstrates, often results in some form of countermoves by others, usually competitive in appearance and intended to be cancelling or offsetting.

Occasionally, it becomes necessary to reexamine the goals or the settings of a system with an eye to changing them. When opposition parties come to power, it has been noted, they may suddenly find themselves confronted with the incompatability of their previous goals with the feedback they now receive from the society at large. As a consequence, new parties in power can find themselves responding to these pressures by changing their own professed goals rather than those of the government. *Goal-changing feedback* reveals its more general role in preserving continuity and stability in the larger social system through altering the goals or settings of significant social groups within it.[8]

1.4.2 Multilateral Feedback – Ruben

Brent Ruben has drawn an important distinction between the use of the concept of feedback to describe one-way relationships (essentially the monitoring process in a cause-effect relationship such as that of the thermostat on a furnace or airconditioner) and its use in describing reciprocal relationships.[9] Since human communication normally involves the interaction of two or more persons, it is perhaps the best example of reciprocal or multilateral relationships. The concept of *multilateral feedback* describes this give and take in human relationships by emphasizing that what is feedback to one person is feed forward to the other. Ruben notes that the failure to think in terms of this give and take leads to what might be called *the effective fallacy* – the belief on the part of teachers, say, that what the student learns is exactly what the teacher intends. A fuller appreciation of how human interaction stresses multilateral and negotiated forms of feedback is an important matter and the subject of the chapter to follow.

CHAPTER 2

Interdependency and Human Needs

2.1 The Reduction of Uncertainty

2.1.1 Escaping Anxiety

We need to communicate and we need to be communicated with as well. By learning to express our needs we gradually enter into a complex of human relations, where the possibility of trust, agreement, cooperation – and their opposites – demands that we assign values to the various practical expressions of these needs. The idea of describing human kind as a collection of needs and values interacting with the reality around us is a controversial one. According to the theory, if we were left without suitable restraints, our interaction with the world around us would soon generate instabilities and disequilibrium in response to the complexity of that world; and this, in turn, would create increasing tension in the individual. Several pioneering thinkers about the communication process have proposed that the patterns and varieties of interpretations and actions that we do develop in dealing with our own realities are, therefore, the outgrowth of efforts to reduce these tensions.

This may seem somewhat limited as a description. Human activity, afterall, must be more than strategies for reducing the uncertainties produced by the reality we perceive about us. Yet, these strategies do provide a rough analogy to feedback as a process through which humans, not unlike other organisms, continuously stabilize their ongoing relationship to a world of uncertainties. And, as we shall see, some far-reaching revisions have arisen out of this provocative hypothesis.

2.1.2 The Natural Attitude – Schutz

Occasionally our status as independent agents in the world runs up against the shadow world of our illusions. All of us, from time to time, have had experience with the disorientations which can result when support for our interpretations of reality is threatened or withdrawn. And yet the very fact that such disorientations are exceptions seems to underscore our shared faith that there is some constant and reliable reality "out there." The sociologist Alfred Schutz called this unquestioning sense we have of our reality *the natural attitude.* With it we feel the coherence of the world about us and the unity of ourselves as active participants in that world. Without it, we can find ourselves thrown into confusion and crisis.[1]

2.1.3 Support of the Natural Attitude – the Asch experiments

A student is the last to enter a room where the professor has asked for participants in an experiment on visual perception. The task is to compare the lengths of lines and to identify those lines which are identical. All proceeds unanimously for a time. Then suddenly on one of the cards the last student finds himself in opposition to all the others on the length of one line. The student is incredulous; there is the clear evidence of his senses. On subsequent trials he disagrees again – and again the others line up unanimously against his judgment. What the student does not know is that he alone is the subject of the experiment, the others having been briefed beforehand to systematically disagree with his responses. At this point the lone dissenter often experiences doubt and confusion; he may hesitate a long time before answering. And inevitably some dissenters will submit to the judgment of the others, in the face of their own contradictory perceptual evidence.

In experiments of this sort conducted at the University of

Pennsylvania Solomon Asch put many individuals in a position of radical conflict with all other members of a group to test the psychological consequences. Surprisingly, in a third of the experiments the lone subject came around to agree with the group opinion against the evidence of his own senses. Asch called this *the majority effect,* a measurement of the frequency of errors in the direction of the distorted estimates of the majority. Perhaps more ominous was the fact that of the other remaining dissenters about one third "tended toward" the majority position. Only one quarter remained completely independent – in support of what they had actually seen.[2]

At the conclusion of each experiment, the independent dissenters admitted to strong feelings of self-doubt and uncertainty about what had been experienced. Some whimsically reported thoughts of having their eyes checked. And one lovely died-in-the-wool independent reported that he had thought the others subject to an experimental illusion to which he was not. For those who yielded to the majority view, Asch described three main consequences: distortion of perception, distortion of judgment, distortion of action. Interestingly, only when one or two others supported the dissenter's judgment did the rate of submission to the majority drop below a third. The natural attitude, it would seem, needs supportive company. When we don't get it for the reality we perceive, we may opt for the group illusion.

It should be noted that it is difficult, if not impossible, to design experiments of this sort without resorting to some kind of trick to elicit the type of responses required. Perhaps this is why variations on such experiments are seldom successfully repeated on the same subjects.

2.2 Dissonance Reduction

2.2.1 Cognitive Dissonance – Festinger

In his studies of decision-making, Leon Festinger noted that, after making decisions, people tend to remain loyal to their choices.[3] Children prefer the toys they have chosen over the ones they have rejected, much as drivers tend to continue to prefer the cars they buy over those they don't. However, when it becomes difficult to remain loyal to our choices, when things happen to contradict our expectations, or when expectations are not fulfilled, the result is what Festinger calls *cognitive dissonance.* Cognitive dissonance refers to situations, experimental and actual, which do not fulfill our normal expectations.

Dissonance normally results from finding oneself in the wrong regarding some set of decisions or assumptions one had previously made. And since "loyalty to choice" usually prevails, the tendency of both individuals and groups is, firstly, to attempt to reduce the dissonance rather than to change beliefs or behaviors. Thus, Festinger found that students who were persuaded to tell other students that a boring experiment was really fun experienced dissonance. Some of the students were paid $1.00 to do the persuading and some were paid $10.00. Those who were paid $1.00 essentially to lie to other students – and who therefore appeared to have less justification for doing so – experienced the most dissonance, which they attempted to reduce by coming around to regard the experiment as really fun after all.

In more extreme situations, such as the occasional discovery of Japanese soldiers still hiding out on remote Pacific islands in the belief that it was their duty to the Emperor not to surrender, dissonance reduction may take on bizarre characteristics. When questioned, such soldiers have insisted that since they received no orders in their isolated outposts they simply chose to continue in a way that preserved their increasingly fragile sense of reality. It is sometimes easier to deny the obvious than to abandon the support ones reality provides. This is even more graphic in the case of those religious sects in Japan whose members, after the conclusion of the war, continued to believe the defeat of the Japanese Empire to be a conspiracy and a hoax, presumably because nothing in their system of beliefs allowed them to account for the meaning and the consequences of such a defeat. In the aftermath of a decision dissonance reduction refers to an increase in the desirability of a chosen alternative and a decrease in the desirability of a rejected one. At the extremes, it seems, our versions of reality cannot be easily disentangled from the company we keep.

2.2.2 Consonance

It is somewhat of a truism among social scientists that it is easier for someone to accept new facts than it is for them to accept new opinions. So when a group of social psychologists in the early sixties set out to examine how people with varying degrees of racial prejudice interpreted a film, *Home of the Brave,* in which the roles and relations of whites and blacks were unconventionally treated (at least for that time period), the results suggested some parallels with those of Festinger. The researchers found that viewers with inflexible attitudes and values initially were thrown into conflict by the unconventional roles of the blacks and whites they saw portrayed. These same viewers were able to reduce this conflict not by altering their beliefs or opinions but by concentrating on other aspects of the film's content.[4] When faced with things that run counter to our deep-seated expectations, it would seem that we first try to direct our attention to those things with which our beliefs are *consonant.*

Social psychologists generally believe that consonance influences our interpretation of events, especially disturbing events, by directing those interpretations in one of two ways: toward *identification,* when the belief structures offered through the event and those of the interpreter are not significantly in conflict; and toward *projection,* when the interpreter is able to refashion the content of an event in a manner consistent with his dominant beliefs. When efforts are made to structure content for large numbers of people with diverse beliefs and preferences – as is the case with virtually all conventional forms of mass-produced communication – it is worth emphasizing that this structured content is always subject to interpretation from the standpoint of the needs and values of the interpreter. It is only common sense to make the observation that content is continuously qualified by the relationship that we have toward it. However, the relationship between the senders of messages and the receivers of messages (one of the "common sense" ways of describing the communication process) is a complex one, and it is unlikely that we can grasp the consequences of such messages for others from our own direct observations of the message content alone.

2.2.3 Manipulation of the Natural Attitude

2.2.3.1 The Prisoners' Dilemma – Tucker

In the 1950s a mathematics professor at Princeton University, Albert Tucker, published a tantalizing formulation for what can happen to the natural attitude when doubt about the nature of a relationship between people is introduced by a third party. Tucker labelled it the prisoners' dilemma, and it has since become a significant puzzle, especially for those concerned with the manipulation of decision-making.[5] In the original version two men suspected of armed robbery are brought before a prosecuting attorney. The prosecutor explains to them that, while he is completely convinced of their guilt, he does not have sufficient evidence to convict them. Instead he offers them a deal. He can, he reminds them, send them to jail for six months in any case for the lesser offense of possessing fire arms. Or, if they both agree to confess to the burglary, he offers them each the minimum sentence of two years. Think about it, he says, and he adds a qualifier: should only one of you confess, that person will become a witness for the state and go free, while the other will receive the maximum sentence of twenty years. Whereupon, much to their consternation, the two prisoners are escorted away to separate cells and further communication between them is suspended. Denied contact with one another and forced to make a decision that involves them both, each prisoner must think through his options and ponder his relationship to the other. In effect, each must continue to construct both sides of their relationship, to argue both points of view. At first it is obvious that they both should remain silent and go to jail for six months; but this is soon transformed into speculations on the relationship with the other, on trustworthiness, even on the prospect of a lengthy jail term. And once the prisoner finds himself slipping into thinking in these terms, he must begin to wonder if his partner in crime can be thinking these things too. And if he is thinking of his partner thinking in this way, what can his partner be thinking? And so on, until, before long, each prisoner should either be climbing the walls with anxiety about his partner or breaking them down with newfound enthusiasm for true confessions – in the latter case, of course, ending up at the prosecutor's mercy.

The predicament, according to Professor Tucker, has no formal solution, and, it should be humanely noted, thus far no documented applications to criminal justice. It does, however, suggest that matters of mutual trust and cooperation depend upon the give and take of interpersonal communication, especially, it would seem, among thieves.

2.2.3.2 Conflict and Cooperation

The conflict experiments of Kurt Lewin provide an interesting footnote to the experiments of Asch and Tucker. In Lewin's Robber's Cave experiments, young boys were divided into arbitrary units in summer camp and, by sometimes subtle and sometimes not so subtle interventions on the part of the camp "instructors," soon found themselves transformed into hostile groups who taunted each other continually. Subsequent efforts on the part of the instructors to get the two groups to "relate" resulted in even worse tensions between them. Only when a series of artificial crises were created, which could be remedied only if both sides pooled their efforts and cooperated, did the conflict abate. A break in the camp's water supply, for instance, was one of a number of problems requiring a collective effort that brought the two groups back together.[6]

Experiments are one thing and actual circumstances are another, but Edgar J. Friedenberg has noted in his studies of the penitentiary system in Canada and the United States that the relations between prisoners and guards is characterized by similar sorts of induced hostilities.[7] In fact, efforts at improving relations between these two groups – as Lewin's experiments might lead us to expect – as often as not exacerbate the conflict between them. Cooperation and collective effort, Friedenberg observes, often depend upon the perception of common problems, often in spite of the many efforts to manipulate the "natural attitude."

2.3 Bounded Rationality

2.3.1 Prisoners of Experience – Kunreuther

It would seem that some things, even in an imperfect world, should be obvious to everyone and, therefore, matters on which we could all agree – like not throwing stones if you live in glass houses, or having flood insurance if you live on the flood plain. Not so. In fact, Kunreuther found that people living in such hazard-susceptible areas as flood plains and earthquake zones have little knowledge about these hazards or the options for protecting themselves.[8] Such people suffer from another kind of dilemma. Of the flood plain inhabitants Kunreuther studied, most had neither purchased insurance nor flood-proofed their structures with special materials, although both were subsidized and readily available. A few, who had previous experience with floods, had insurance; a few more had insurance because their neighbors had insurance. Perhaps more significant Kunreuther found that people were unable to venture a guess at the likelihood of a future flood. Many, it seemed, had never thought about the consequences of a potential disaster – at least not until Kunreuther showed up. Man may be a betting animal, but on low probability events he is not much of a handicapper.

Using the classical notion of decision-making where one rationally chooses among fixed and known alternatives, each with known consequences, Kunreuther found it impossible to account for the behavior of his homeowners. Instead he offered an alternative explanation. If an individual has too little knowledge, or if the personal costs involved in getting the necessary knowledge are simply too great, that individual will probably rely on his neighbors experience and his own. A person who has had previous experience with floods or has neighbors who have insured themselves may act on that knowledge to protect himself. This is sometimes meanly referred to as the influence of the *regret factor.*

Kunreuther studied the residents of earthquake zones with much the same result. In the face of limited knowledge of low probability events, the regret factor seems to have more impact than other sources of information, whether graphically filmed documentaries, advertising campaigns, newscasts, insurance agents, or disturbing visits from the social scientist.

2.3.2 Informational Inequality

The winner of the 1978 Nobel Prize in economics Herbert Simon has observed that, for the most part, modern man operates under severe cognitive limitations, limitations created by unequal access to information (and discussion) and limitations that result from our beliefs, our personal circles, and our affiliations.[9] Because these limitations would seem to be the rule and not the exception, Simon believes that we should not be so surprised when people form simplified views of the world and overly simplified plans of action. Moreover, we should expect that there will be active efforts on the part of some to take advantage of this state of affairs – to promote simplified models and to attempt to manipulate opinion and behavior in the same manner. In fact, much that has been examined in this chapter underscores the way in which limitations are placed upon our judgments and actions by the interdependent character of the natural attitude. Both the certainties and the uncertainties of reality, we could say, are in part the product of these interdependencies. The following chapter examines the role of symbolic communication in the production and maintenance of this interdependent reality.

CHAPTER 3

Reflexion and the Social Order

3.1 Symbolic Interaction

In our experiencing of the world we can never bypass the symbolic process. The world that emerges through our experience and our interpretations is a "constructed" rather than a "given" reality. We continuously produce meaning about this world somewhat the way a cartographer maps out a territory. In observing our reality, we are limited by the language we use to describe it; and that language, in turn, is limited by the requirement of its communicability to others. The end product of a cartographer's work may need only be meaningful to the community of other experts through a shared scientific code; or, by contrast, it may have to be made comprehensible to a broader and less expert public. It is in somewhat the same way that our private *subjective* experiences are, through symbols, transformed into communicable or *intersubjective* ones. Our experiences gain *coherence* through the symbolic system we use to order them into perceptions and interpretations and *meaningfulness* by being successfully communicated to others.

This is the process by which we become located within symbolic reality. Each biological individual must be progressively drawn away from the animal nature which dominates his infancy and into the social nature of society. Society engineers the process by systematically providing its members with a linguistic-symbolic system through which the instinctual and the social are split – and through which the individual is trained to prefer the latter. Hanley Shands calls this process schizogenesis, an inelegant term for the way in which society is able to split the biological creature into dual aspects potentially in conflict.[1] The tension generated by these two aspects, or natures, can resolve itself integratively or disintegratively. In the former case we get approximations of civilization; in the latter case the symptoms of mental disorder.

As children grow and develop within a particular linguistic-symbolic world, they find that language comes to refer less and less to specific objects and their need or demand for them, and more and more to broad categories of experience. As language becomes independent of the world of objects, a child begins to experience the first of its socializing power. The first words of an infant demonstrate its own power over the environment because they elicit actions from others. Words seem to behave like stimuli that bring responses – mothers with food or fathers with attention. Of course, with some luck this may continue, but the child as he continues to acquire language becomes aware of a new pattern encompassing the old one. The words and gestures that formerly demonstrated power over others, he begins to see, elicit also a profound influence over himself. When words and gestures in this manner come to elicit or "call out" responses in the individual himself at the same time they call out responses in others the socializing power of language is set in place. All of us can glimpse this power by observing children "playing" at the roles of doctor, homemaker, soldier. Such forms of play seem to draw out of children the enactment of adult roles almost exclusively through the mimicry of key words and gestures. The pioneer social psychologist George Herbert Mead, early in the twentieth century, identified this socializing power of language and gesture as the role of the *significant symbol.*[2] As we mature, Mead believed, certain roles and relationships become significant for us; and it is these significant symbols which continue to draw out of us the enactment of a variety of social roles. Though Mead did not explore all the ways society influences this process, he felt that the choice of significant symbols in the socialization process – sociation as he called it – helped explain the process whereby men and women evolved into a variety of continuously changing social roles. Through the mediation of significant symbols this could be accomplished in society without the need to resort continually to authoritarian measures (threats of violence), or to coercion (violence itself).

In demonstrating how the integration of individuals into the social order might be *steered* and *stabilized* through these sorts of symbolic interactions with ourselves and with others, Mead contributed another concept as fundamental to understanding the process of communication as that of feedback – the concept of *reflexivity*.

3.2 Reflexivity

3.2.1 Seeing, Speaking, and Writing

The mapping of our experiences in terms of some symbolic order allows us to distinguish between ourselves as subjects and a world of objects. When we enter into relationships with others, our words and gestures become part of the world of symbolic objects, whose impact and received meaning in other people we can observe. Because as subjects we can also attempt to take the position of others and to see ourselves and our actions from that perspective, we can not only observe but anticipate their reactions to us. This capacity to see ourselves as others see us, while still simultaneously remaining in a relationship with them, is what is called reflexivity. Reflexivity does not refer to the accuracy of what we see when we try to take the position of others with regard to ourselves, but the general self-regarding or self-monitoring activity itself. The following examples indicate just how profoundly reflexivity influences three primary modes of interaction – those of seeing, speaking, and writing.

3.2.2 Seeing

Von Senden observed that congenitally blind people whose sight is restored to them through cataract operations frequently have the experience of feeling ashamed when they discover for the first time how their actions can be observed continuously and in minute detail without the necessity of physical contact.[3] Since they can now do with their eyes what formerly they could do only with the fingertips, the mode of visual space makes it not only possible but obligatory for them to regard themselves as others see them. To experience oneself from the point of view of others – to take, as it were, the position of others with regard to oneself – appears to be central to that uniquely interactive process through which we come to identify ourselves as having and playing a role in society.

3.2.3 Speaking

Dance and Larson describe the function of speaking as a way of linking a person with himself or herself and with others.[4] Though this dual linkage is integrated in mature speech, in the early development of a child's speech patterns there is a sharp distinction between *egocentric speech* – that is, speech that is no more than the vocalization of the child's private communication with himself – and *nonegocentric speech,* when the child acquires the capability to "tailor" his messages in ways which take account of others, whom he now recognizes as different from himself. The transition from vocalized inner speech to speech directed to others provides a basis for all subsequent development of communication skills. It would seem that this decentering of the speech process from egocentric to nonegocentric is a necessary condition for acquiring reflexivity. In this way, Dance and Larson believe, children help socialize themselves, literally by talking themselves into their own maturity.

3.2.4 Writing

Much writing is directed at specific persons whose possible responses can be anticipated and whose feedback, in any case, may arrive by return mail. But the more immediate features of the writing process involve an internalization of this relationship between oneself and others, where the thinking through and revising of the writer in response to the feedback of some imagined reader seems to approximate an entire system of communicating with oneself. As we acquire the capacity for written language a new and different system of inner speech is generated which Hanley Shands calls *reflexive contemplation.*[5] In written language – and in other visual and aural media – the relationship between the individual writing and the outside world is partly disregarded. The act of acquiring written language, whether by the individual in his personal development or historically as it has been acquired by entire cultures and societies, represents a profound transformation of the system of inner speech.

These thoughts on the role and function of reflexivity in our social communication are complex and deserve recapitulation. Because we can transform our experience of the world symbolically, we can create distance from that world. We can take the position of others with regard to ourselves, we can consider alternatives, project the consequences of different courses of action, and in these ways we can break the hold that the present moment and our immediately given experience would otherwise have over us. This ability to contemplate our social world in relation to ourselves and others frees us temporarily from the link between organism and environment. It is our capacity for reflexion that allows us to break the link with an immediately given environment and thereby to anticipate and plan without the risks of action. And it is our capacity for reflexion in conjunction with our mastery of symbolic communication that allows us to construct our own identity through exploring a diversity of roles both real and imagined. Reflexivity thus describes the symbolic process by which we come to be able to interpret and to stabilize our experience of an uncertain social reality around us.

3.3 Social Consensus

3.3.1 Working Consensus – Goffman

In the same way that reflexion can help us appreciate the steering and stabilizing of the self in relation to social roles, it can also help us understand the steering and stabilizing of the social roles themselves. Social roles are not something that we automatically fit into. Like theatrical roles they must be worked out and performed, with parts or routines, audiences, observers and co-participants – and always with more or less success. Erving Goffman defines such performances of roles "as the enactment of rights and duties attached to a given status (where) a social role will involve one or more parts and . . . each of these different parts may be presented by the performer on a series of occasions to the same kinds of audience or to an audience of the same persons."[6] In defining a social role it is usually in the interest of an individual to present himself in such a way as to influence the response of others. *Influencing the definition of the situation,* as Goffman calls it, seems to involve two different types of activity: firstly, the expressions the individual makes, mainly his verbal assertions, and secondly, the expressions he gives off. Normally the verbal activity is more controllable and therefore Goffman believes it is the other less controllable behaviour that accompanies talk which, especially in initial encounters, is used by others to "check up" on what is said. It is, of course, possible to convey misinformation through both types of communication – by *deceit* in the verbal mode and by *feigning* in the nonverbal mode.

Through the defining of situations a great variety of social roles and relationships are continually reproduced. Goffman refers to this process as the formation of a *working consensus.* Two friends meeting in public will tend to show reciprocal affection and concern, whereas a specialist in a service occupation such as a physician or therapist will attempt to maintain a disinterested involvement with a client who, in return, will defer to the competency of the specialist. In each case the working consensus is not to be found in the polite "greetings" of the friends or the surface "deference" of the client and the "detachment" of the specialist, but in the deeper concerns for friendship or for the client's problems. In this sense, social roles are always in the process of being worked out and performed; and the authenticity of these roles is continuously negotiated and monitored every time we interact. By this process, social roles come to exert changing demands on the individuals who perform them, and through this extended process society comes to exert changing demands upon the social roles themselves.

3.3.2 Foreground and Background Consensus – Habermas

In situations where more substantive agreements must be mutually worked out there is usually some sort of point counterpoint. We take sides, we criticize, often we play act as a means of testing or provoking. When agreement lags we can call in others to give advice or adjudicate; we can agree to disagree. Occasionally we must resort to more formal authority and see a lawyer, or a therapist, or mother. All this is possible because we accept limitations on our disputes and we recognize, at least implicitly, the appropriateness of resolving differences in certain ways. There are rules of the game. We tend to reach for the telephone before reaching for the revolver; and we accept the role of the courts even when we are not satisfied with their decisions. These rules and the institutions that back them up constitute an important part of our symbolic social order. As we mature such rules and institutions come to exert a significant regulative influence upon us. The sociologist Jürgen Habermas characterizes this influence according to the type of agreement that is promoted. The two most general types consist of those rules and institutions that promote a foreground consensus and those that promote a background consensus.[7]

A *foreground consensus* includes all those interpersonal arrangements that characterize our everyday life, economic transactions, personal relationships, and so on. Yet in each case of forming a foreground consensus we are aided and abetted by a large number of conventions, rules of behavior, laws, by-laws and standard procedures. These shared values or ways of doing things are what Habermas calls a *background consensus;* and it is because these shared ideas exist in our background that foreground agreements are possible. There may be differences in customs and beliefs among societies, but the role of the foreground and background consensus Habermas finds to be nearly universally present in modern societies.

Only when a background consensus is popularly questioned, it seems, does the possibility for major, even radical, change in a social order emerge. The process of making or amending the constitutions of modern states conveys much of the symbolic power and high drama associated with changes in a background consensus. At such moments everyone must consider the consequences of the change. In a sense, people must project themselves beyond the proposed change and from that hypothetical vantage point consider the implications for themselves and for others. The decisions in our own century to provide universal suffrage (the extension of the right to vote to virtually all adult members of a society) involved far-reaching changes in attitudes on the part of many. Yet, this decision was itself the result of attitudes which had already changed to such an extent that the background consensus "limiting" universal suffrage had begun to break down. To many the denial of voting rights to others had ceased to be a shared value. In our own century, universal suffrage is a classic example of how the steering and stabilizing of roles and rules of the game in society occasionally may require profound changes in our political rules and institutions. From the point of view of this chapter, we could say that significant symbols also exert an important influence on the continuous reworking of the social order. Significant symbols and our reflexive relation to them play an important role in the production of our interdependent social reality.

3.3.3 The Prisoners' Dilemma Revisited

The role of reflexion compares in an interesting way with Professor Tucker's dilemma. Tucker's prisoners, presented with the task of reaching an agreement and maintaining a consensus about it, found themselves in a less than ideal situation to do this and governed by a rule that forebade communication between them. Denied direct interaction with each other, each prisoner had to work out this otherwise mutual course of action by himself. Each attempted to do so by trying to see himself as the other saw him, taking the role of the other with regard to himself. But in the absence of any sort of information feedback about what was *actually* happening, this reflexive *role-taking* on the part of the prisoners, rather than stabilizing their relationship, actually worked to undermine it. Our agreements and the conditions under which we reach those agreements are always contingent. The formation of our everyday agreements, or even our broadest social consensuses, will depend in part upon the conditions of communication, actual and perceived. We could say they are not only interdependent; they are reflexively related.

3.4 Conclusion

Feedback and reflexion are intertwined aspects of all human communication. If in these first chapters we have separated them, it has been to make clearer their significance to the communication process. Information feedback and reflexive role-taking are fundamentals of that process. The following chapter offers a recapitulation of their importance, and some further indication of why both concepts remain essential to the analysis of communication phenomena.

CHAPTER 4

Modes of Human Communication

4.1 Mr. Tylor's Science

4.1.1 Culture and Communication

As a young man Edward Tylor had been advised to travel in warm climates for reasons of health. He took the advice, travelled through Mexico in the 1860s, survived his ill health and was served well by the experience. In the following decade, from his home in England Edward Tylor put together a range of ideas relating to earlier civilizations that had begun to coalesce for him during his Mexican travels; and in 1856 he published *Researches into the Early History of Mankind,* a book in some ways equivalent to Darwin's *Origin of the Species* in that it sets out the mandate for a new science, the science of culture.[1]

Tylor's science of culture begins with a clear central premise: that in order for people to communicate there must be *repeated activities* and *shared ideas.* His claim that repeated activities and shared ideas were the fundamentals of communication is possibly the earliest recognition we have of the regulative or stabilizing function that communication plays in culture. In fact, Tylor's central premise anticipates by half a century what we previously noted as the central theme of communication research in the twentieth century – that is, the way in which the steering and stabilizing of man in society depends in part upon the role of communication.

There are, in fact, some striking analogies between the central premise of Tylor's science and the modern concepts of feedback and reflexion. In communication involving two or more individuals, feedback links describe not only a way of detecting and correcting deviations from previous performances; feedback links also provide a description of the ongoing mutuality of the relationships built up and maintained between people or between people and their social environment. *Interactive feedback,* as it might be relabelled, seems to be analogous to Tylor's emphasis on the role of repeated activities.

By contrast, reflexion emphasizes our human social ability to consider things from the point of view of others – and therefore to see the way in which we ourselves and our ideas are perceived by those around us. Reflexion is a sort of projective or imaginary feedback (by comparison to feedback about what actually happens) that helps us generate options for future behavior. *Reflexive interaction* allows us to act on how we think things are perceived by others to sustain their perceptions; and contrarily, it allows us to consider the consequences of acting in ways that attempt to alter or correct these perceptions on the part of others. But perhaps the most important function of reflexion is to provide us with the capacity to share our experiences and feelings with others – and to know with some certainty that the matters we refer to, like Tylor's concept of "shared ideas," is something familiar to us both.

4.1.2 Modes of Communication

When Tylor tried to explain how it was that the repeated activities and shared ideas which made up a culture came about – and even more crucially how it was that they changed – he stressed the importance of the various modes or systems of communication. Tylor was not trying to downplay the importance of material circumstances (drought, plague, war, invention, economics and politics); but he was trying to underscore the sense in which the modes or systems of communication that a culture adopted were also a part of its material circumstance. Tylor identified a number of what might be called *primary modes of communication* that he believed to be *nearly universally present* in early cultures: gestures, languages, various types of notation for counting and classification, myths, story-telling, and dance. All these modes serve as a means for face-to-face interaction and as a means for disseminating information and ideas throughout a culture. Modes both facilitate and limit communication. They facilitate *what* a culture might express and they limit *how* a culture might produce that expression. By his emphasis on the modes of communication, Tylor gave us one of the earliest indications of the role that changing modes of communication might play in the development of our different civilizations, with their different beliefs and practices.

4.2 Technologies of the Intellect

4.2.1 Systems of Communicative Acts – Goody

Most of us have some grasp of the role that the modes of communication have played in the fashioning of cultures and their development. We are accustomed to thinking of language, systems of notation, writing, printing, broadcasting and computing as ways in which communication is enhanced, improved and facilitated. We appreciate how the absence of a mode creates a limitation on expression. We can understand, for instance, the problems the deaf must have in communicating without speech in an oral-aural society; or the way in which the illiterate are limited in a literate world. Additionally, most of us have had the experience of acquiring the skill to use and comprehend these modes ourselves – to speak languages, to read and write, even to program. We know firsthand the differences these modes make in the type and the extent of expression available to us.

The anthropologist Jack Goody has called all of these modes of communication the technologies of the intellect.[2] The introduction of new modes into a culture or society through the teaching of skills and the technological means have very real consequences in that they bring about changes in what he calls *the system of communicative acts.* In the development of modern states, the growth of bureaucracies depends upon the ability to control people indirectly by means of written communication; and the growth of bureaucracies lessens the need for direct control over people and, in turn, reduces the importance of face-to-face forms of control. The introduction of writing (and literacy) thus brings about changes in the system of communicative acts whereby new types of communicative acts and social relations are now possible and older types of communicative acts and social relations are no longer as necessary. The interdependence of writing and bureaucratic practices also provides us with a remarkable example of how new modes of communication (and the acquisition of the skills and materials necessary to use them) both enable and constrain the development of repeated activities and shared ideas in a culture.

4.2.2 Modes, Means and Media

The term just introduced is a possible source of confusion. A mode makes possible a system of communicative acts; those we have mentioned include gestures, languages, notation and classification systems, writing, as well as computational schemes and programs. Medium normally refers only to the material conditions of communication, the hardware involved, such as paper, broadcast equipment, and terminals. Means of communication refers, although not consistently, to the availability of skills and organization as well as the hardware itself. The latter usage is not consistent among scholars and practitioners, in part because the term "means" is a common noun with a variety of everyday usages. In the present text, mode is the more significant term because it refers to the way in which something is done – specific systems of communicative acts (repeated activities) and the specific types of meanings (shared ideas) associated with them. Media, of course, refers to mass communication systems – their organization, hardware, and messages.

4.3 A Note on Methods and the Interpretation of Meaning

4.3.1 Direct Observation and Pragmatic Understanding – Morris

Almost a half century ago a University of Chicago philosopher, Charles Morris, pointed out in graphic terms the very substantial problems that exist for us whenever and wherever we attempt to account for the meaning that communicative actions have for others.[3]

Certain communicative actions can be understood through *direct observation,* where the purpose or meaning of the event is immediately apparent, such as regular changes to the environment, habitual behavior in animals, or repeated activities of a clearly defined sort – the play of children or daily routines of adults. Acts or events which hold direct observational meaning Morris labelled as having *denotative meaning.*

Other communicative actions, even at times the ones noted above, are more opaque, resistant to such direct and immediate understanding. When this is the case, the situation demands what might be called a *pragmatic understanding,* where the motivation or the "cause" of an act or event can be grasped only by placing it in a more inclusive context of meaning. Acts or events which necessitate a pragmatic understanding Morris labelled as having *significative meaning.*

The "sign" of the Christian cross is an example that might make this distinction a little clearer.

(1) If an animal responds to a cross in a laboratory context, we could say that it is conditioned to do so, as if it were a mechanical reaction. At this level of observation the interaction between animal and cross has an immediately apparent meaning. The cross is a "signal" to the animal and the context is unambiguous, if a bit contrived.

(2) If a mature person responds to the cross, we could say that he does so in the context of its history as a religious symbol, which he recognizes in his own way and not necessarily as a cue for one sort of direct or immediate response. The cross is a "symbol" to the respondent; hence understanding what motivates his or her response demands a more inclusive context

of meaning.

(3) If a young child responds to the cross, it may be doing so with some recognition of the immediate interpersonal context, perhaps as an imitation of the actions of others but without necessarily comprehending its symbolic importance. In this case there seems to be both signal-meaning and symbol-meaning; hence the likelihood that both direct observation and pragmatic understanding could provide *complementary* ways of grasping the meaning involved.[4]

Denotative meanings (signal meanings) can be produced and observed on all levels of biological life; whereas significative meanings (symbol-meanings) are produced and understood only through the complex web of human society.

4.3.2 Objective Meaning and Subjective Meaning – Langer

Susanne Langer, a philosopher of language concerned with the problems of pragmatic understanding, characterized the difficulties of grasping the meaning of communicative acts and events in this way: it is one thing to explain the repeated activities of the lower animals in terms of the signals that govern their relationship to the environment (objective meaning). But can we really explain in this same way the dancing or praying of human beings before some totem, ancient or modern, for thousands of years? And even if we could, just how much would we actually have explained about the motivation or the cause of it? After all, even rats and morons would learn to question the results of such repeated activity faster than that. The deeper meaning of such acts and events requires that we understand something about people's relationships to each other and their shared ideas about this system or constellation of communicative acts.[5]

A pragmatic understanding requires that we approach the subjective meaning of communicative acts and events in two ways: (1) through describing the actual interactions of some individual or group (direct observation); and (2) through theoretically constructing a pattern of interaction which can then be ascribed to these individuals or groups. The difficulties involved in doing this sort of analysis are considerable; our perceptions and interpretations of others may be in error through the influence of our different beliefs and preferences, or by the carefulness and completeness of our observations, or even by unacknowledged social and cultural difficulties with those with whom we are dealing.

If this seems to present maddening difficulties, Langer reminds us that the real complexity of our communicative acts and the social realities produced through them may lie precisely here, in what the previous chapter identified as its symbolic and reflexive dimension.

4.4 An Introductory Conclusion

Much that follows in this book is intended to clarify what is meant by *the mode of communication.* The concepts of feedback and reflexion provide an introductory example of how the mode of communication can be identified and analyzed. It should be repeated that techniques of inquiry, whether direct observation or pragmatic understanding, and techniques of interpretation, whether for objective or subjective meaning, all depend upon concepts such as these.

In the next few chapters another concept is highlighted, a concept that has been in some ways as much a barrier to conceptual-theoretical progress as a facilitator of it, *the concept of information.* For half a century now there have been serious and enthusiastic efforts to conceive of all types of communication as forms of information exchange. By now there are some deep divisions of opinion over just what is meant by the terms information and exchange and just how they ought to be investigated. Precisely because the concept of information has had such an influence upon our past understanding of communication and because there have been so many questions raised about the intellectual and practical inadequacies of the information concept of communication, we need to treat the matter with caution. These next chapters provide a limited background and discussion of this most controversial of concepts. And just for the record, it should be said that inadequate concepts can and do provide insight, often inadvertently.

PART TWO

The Empirical Enclosures — Modes of Reality Integration

Much that inspired the study of communication began in Chicago. There in the first decades of the century many matters that would come to dominate our epoch were already in evidence. The mythic American frontier had been declared officially closed after the census of 1896; trains ran regularly to and from the hinterlands of the west. At the Chicago Exposition the Yugoslavian-born inventor Nicola Tesla had demonstrated the future of electricity with his dynamo and lighting displays, a future boosted by Marconi's successful radio transmissions across the North Atlantic. The technologies for motion pictures and lithography stood poised for development. The telephone was much in demand; even the possibility of television and facsimile reproduction had been foreseen.

In the closing circle of the American frontier these things fed back on the burgeoning mid-western capital with a firm assurance that, if one form of life and community seemed to be waning before this new infrastructure of transportation and communication, another form was emerging through these same developments. There was, after all, University of Chicago philosopher John Dewey observed, the stable community of science and the critical resources of a political democracy to provide the necessary guidance. The future that presented itself to those prescient souls at Chicago on the dawning edge of the century seemed a reasonable and progressive place where communication technology by its capacity to expand the marketplace of ideas could and would broaden the potential for rational thought and reasonable actions.

This spirit of the times and vision of the future, often identified as the progressive era, marks the beginning of a conceptual partnership. Since that time the evolution of human communication has moved in tandem with a succession of technological developments in the communication infrastructure – telephony, lithography, film, broadcasting, and computers. Each of these new technologies at first was perceived to be placing in jeopardy many forms of everyday life where experience was primarily face-to-face and still deeply rooted in local communities. Yet, at least in the eyes of progressives, these new technologies were also establishing new forms of national experience, and in the long run promising to overcome the isolation and distance between communities themselves. In this set of circumstances, it is understandable that the popular concept of communication came to refer to both the flow of ideas and opinion brought about by communication technology and to the direct interaction between people as well. In fact, in these early stages of the rapid technological growth that would engulf the century, midway between the introduction of the telephone and the introduction of radio, it was widely assumed that the crucial limits on experience were those imposed by the *absence* of communication technology.

Since that time we have come to modify and clarify these ideas and expectations about technology and human community, in part through the development of new analytic concepts and in part through sober appraisal of what is meant by that ubiquitous term, information.

CHAPTER 5

The Classical Models of Information

5.1 The Communication Flow Hypotheses

5.1.1 Persuasion – Lasswell

In the 1930s Harold Lasswell proposed that what was important about communicating through the new technologies of mass communication could be found in the answer to a multifaceted question: Who says What in Which channel to Whom with What effect? The 5 Ws gave the first full recognition to the concept of information: what communication media provided was "information" directed to an audience with consequences that could be analyzed and related back to each step in the process. For Lasswell there was little doubt that, in the present century, our media systems would be the primary agencies of social cohesion and linkage to the social environment. All our efforts to plan and coordinate communication through organized technologies were, therefore, matters of power.[1]

Lasswell predicted that specific behavioral effects on individuals and groups could be expected to follow from their encounter with specific contents supplied by the media. By implication, control over the content of communication systems would provide control over these effects. Thus, Lasswell argued that organized forms of communication (such as all forms of modern media) would inevitably be connected to the power structures of society. In stable times, he believed, ruling elites would use communication as a means of preserving the power they had; in times of conflict, the struggle between elites would be in part a struggle for control of the channels of communication themselves.

5.1.2 Gatekeeping – Lewin and White

At about the same time that Lasswell was developing his notions of communication as power, a social psychologist, Kurt Lewin, proposed an hypothesis for how the actual content of media communication was being controlled within the media system itself.[2] As ideas flow through communication channels to consumers, Lewin said, they encounter gates at points along such channels which, in turn, regulate the availability of such materials to those beyond these gates. Lewin argued that by observing the flow of ideas on either side of these gates one could identify the decision-making criteria being used by those who controlled the gates themselves. To the controllers of the gates of media, Lewin gave the now classic label of gatekeepers. It was the gatekeepers, Lewin believed, who held the key to understanding how communication content influenced public behavior.

When David Manning White nearly two decades later took an in-depth look at the editing of an American newspaper, he began with Lewin's two central ideas – that communication flows through specific, identifiable channels and that at points in these channels there are gates which admit or reject specific items.[3] For his gatekeeper, White chose an indulgent, middle-aged, middle-class, mid-western city editor of a mid-sized, mid-western city paper. It was the city editor's job to select or reject news items for each day's paper. White counted what the editor chose and compared them to the totality of items of different sorts that arrived each day (objective criteria). He also talked with and interviewed the editor to find out something of his professed attitudes and beliefs and his general reasons for selecting the news as he did (subjective criteria). White's analysis of the editor's reasons for rejecting various types of news stories indicated a high degree of personal value-judgment. The selection of the news closely reflected the editor's own experiences, attitudes, and expectations – which White found to be typically middle-aged, middle-class, and mid-western. News selection, it seems, is always news selection from some point of view. Perhaps more important was the inference that has been drawn from White's study and that has become a guiding axiom about the media – that what is not communicated may be as significant as what is.

5.1.3 Local Influence – Lazarsfeld, Berelson, Katz

Although the role of gatekeeper has become an important way of talking about social or public communication systems, many questions have been raised about just what kind of control over judgments, opinion, and behavior is exerted by the communication media in this way. There seems to be little doubt that gatekeepers can and do control what is and what is not communicated; but in spite of the many studies of gatekeeper control, an uneasy feeling persisted that by concentrating on the gatekeeping function we might be assuming too narrow a conception about how information actually functioned, and perhaps encouraging a false sense of its effectiveness.

In the 1940s at team of social psychologists and sociologists had begun to propose a modified view. The effects of media, they argued, were rather slight, largely conservative and unlikely to precipitate major changes in either judgment or behavior.[4] Paul Lazarsfeld, Bernard Berelson, and Elihu Katz studied the decision-making process of several American election campaigns over a period of fifteen years. They used the results of their studies to document the process through which media influence choice. The *two-step flow hypothesis*, as it came to be known, states that, especially in the case of political judgment and voting behavior, but also in consumer behavior and professional adoption of new materials and techniques, media information must first pass through opinion leaders, those people regarded as style setters or leaders at the regional or local level and who, in turn, influence directly those around them. If there were gatekeepers within the media deciding what to communicate, those messages still had to pass through the gates of opinion leaders who defined the intellectual, social, and political styles of local groups. It has been noted that all of these flow hypotheses, those flows identified by Lewin and White as well as the modified versions of Lazarsfeld and Katz, do not identify the flow of information per se, but the flow of information and influence as distinct stages of the communication process.

Some corollary support for the interdependency of information and influence came from experimental psychologists at about the same time. Hovland, for example, was able to demonstrate that the recall of factual material fades with time, but initial opinion changes are strengthened when they are in line with prevailing group attitudes. Hovland called this the *sleeper effect.*[5]

In his study of the rise of political figures in the United States, Elihu Katz drew an absurd but telling analogy with patterns that had been observed in the spread of innovative farming techniques: first, local style-setters and innovators, the so-called opinion leaders, are persuaded to endorse a farming technique (or by Katz' application to politics, a political candidate) and then through these opinion leaders a receptivity is created at the local level. Katz made three basic points in reassessing the role of media: first, that mass media dominate society in the production of information, but direct face-to-face interactions play a more significant role in the acceptance of information at the local level. Second, in terms of persuasion the mass media can be more influential in the early informational stages, while personal influence dominates at later stages of decision. And third, opinion leaders themselves are affected primarily not by the mass media but by other opinion leaders, notably those outside their own communities with whom they maintain informal contacts. Together, such findings supported the idea that media information helps reinforce attitudes, opinion, and behavior to a far greater extent than it changes or creates them.[6]

The lengthy history of effects and flow studies has resulted in a number of modifications to the original hypotheses – multi-step flow hypotheses have appeared, even one-step flows have been suggested; and in recent times the flow hypothesis has divided information and influence into two distinctly different types of flow.[7] It would be unkind to pursue it very far, but more than one student forced to contend with this chameleon hypothesis has been driven to wonder whether the professor lecturing him should be viewed as a gatekeeper or an opinion leader; and whether the content being impressed upon him should be seen more as information or personal influence.

5.1.4 A Critique

Early research on the flow and control of information seems to have presented descriptions of control and flow as more or less one-way phenomena from active producers to progressively more passive recipients. Much of this research appears to have slighted the role of the recipients and users of information. Although the work of Lazarsfeld, Berelson, and Katz concentrated on the significance of media information, they also pointed up the significance of personal relations through the role of opinion leaders in the formation of localized opinion. In fact, the concept of opinion leaders today has been replaced by a more detailed emphasis on the significance of the interaction networks and informal commentaries that take place through conversations and familiar contacts. These informal aspects of interaction now appear to many as the primary source of judgments, opinion, and behavior. Media, it is argued, constitute no more than a secondary influence. The Dutch public opinion researcher Martin Brouwer refers to these informal aspects of interaction through what he calls the mycilium analogy, a reference to the thin threads that form the complex underground network by means of which mushrooms spread and from which they break to the surface.[8] There is, Brouwer says, no one opinion that flows, but there are many different publics, a continuous interweaving of communities, groups, and individuals who may come together like the thin threads of mycilium to support an opinion, a decision, or an idea; and who may do so for a variety of reasons and from a great many divergent circumstances.

In a curious way the efforts to define more closely the linkage between mass media, public opinions, and personal actions has achieved something like a demonstration of the opposite. The efforts to define the flow and assess the effects of public media on attitudes, opinions, and actions have given us a convincing demonstration of the differences between the complex give and take of face-to-face relations (with its emphasis on personal and local influence) and the essentially one-way reality of media message transmission (with its emphasis on gatekeeping).

5.2 Mass versus Personal Transactions – Westley and MacLean

Westley and MacLean developed a conceptual distinction between mass and personal modes based upon the notion of sensory field (a reference to the overwhelming quantity of stimuli that comprise the environment at any given time) and the function of intermediary selectors in controlling which and how much material from a sensory field is processed.[9] Their model suggests why face-to-face differs from mass communication in fundamental ways.

Personal communication, they argue, involves more sense modalities and face-to-face relations also provide immediate feedback. In interpersonal acts, more senses (and therefore more kinds of stimuli) can come into play; in interpersonal situations a person has a cross-modality check. Impressions from one sense can be cleared with those received through the other senses. In addition, there is the advantage that comes from knowing the responses of others immediately. Inverting the Westley and MacLean model, we could say that the mass communication mode differs from the personal communication mode in that the number of sense modalities tends to be minimized and orientative feedback is delayed or altogether absent. Their model represents a reasonable and elegant case for viewing these two modes as conceptually distinct forms of communication.

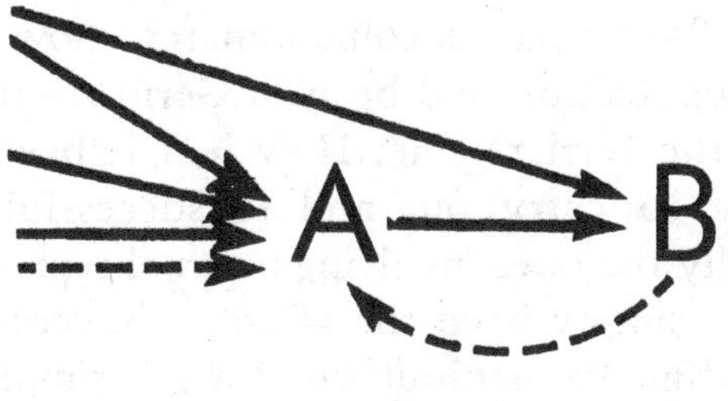

Figure One

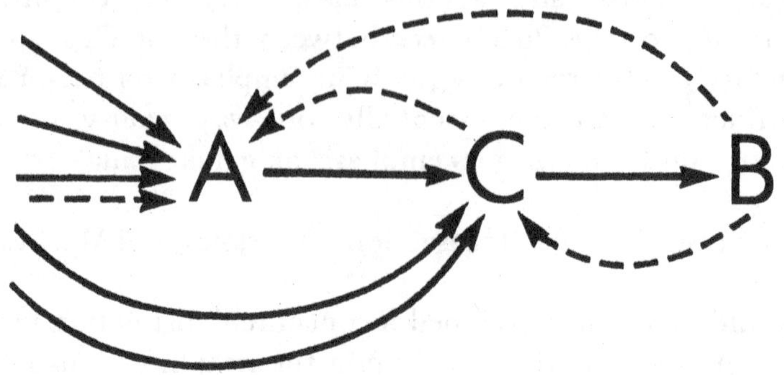

Figure Two

The Transaction Model, Figure One describes a *face-to-face situation* where B may or may not have access to the occurrence or the sensory field to which A's communication refers. Intentionally or unintentionally B provides direct feedback to A. Figure Two refers to the *mass communication situation* where a number of Cs receive from a larger number of As and transmit to very large numbers of Bs, who can also receive from other Cs. The feedback indicated may or may not be present and in any case will likely differ from Figure One in terms of diminished frequency, immediacy, and significance.

5.3 A Postscript on Goebbels' Spies

The line between persuasion and gatekeeping remains difficult to draw with conviction, partly because in our own century propaganda and censorship have lurked in the shadows of both of these activities. The rise of European fascism in the 1930s and the intensive use of modern media for propaganda during the two world wars has provided sobering evidence of potential abuses. To many the Nazi propagandist Josef Goebbels was the extreme example of media misuse.[10] At the Nürnberg Trials which followed the war in 1946 it had become apparent how ineffective any form of public opposition had been in Germany itself in resisting the policies of the Nazi regime. How had it been possible for a civilized society to carry out and to successfully justify such policies, especially the ones involving internal repression of its own citizenry? Had it simply been the effect of successful propaganda and therefore, of media manipulation? Was it simply as many have said the fact of the sword in the background? Goebbels' diaries, which survived the war although he himself did not, provide a complex answer. Goebbels, the master propagandist, was revealed through his diaries to have been a master spy as well. Goebbels had been adept and systematic not only in his use of media, but equally adept and systematic at spying on the German people, sending his operatives incognito into the society at large to test public opinion and to sense the fears and anxieties of people in their daily lives. Through such a system of information feedback Goebbels kept a constant pulse on his propaganda efforts, taking into account the reactions to his various campaigns, modifying tactics, and in general learning to shrewdly manipulate the attitudes (and especially the fears) his informers found already in the public mind.

It is worth underscoring this example with regard to the key distinction in this chapter between mass and personal modes of communication. From the earliest point in this century it was commonly believed that the absence of communication technology placed important limits on face-to-face reality. Communication technologies, progressives believed, held out the possibility of a more rational public. Subsequent studies into the actual flow of information and influence through the mass media systems that developed, especially in the United States, modified this view by distinguishing between the greater significance of mass communication materials in the early informational stages of public awareness and the greater significance of local interpersonal relations at later decision-making stages. Reading the studies of Lazarsfeld, himself a refugee from fascism, and Katz from today's perspective, one can almost sense their relief in finding that local level organization and decision-making had not been eroded by the widespread use of mass communication, especially in its political uses.

Westley and MacLean's model suggests that the persistence of the personal mode for the formation of opinion and judgment may lie in the greater availability of information through other sense modalities and the assurance provided by orientative feedback at the interpersonal level. In most mass communication systems such sense modalities are minimized and orientative feedback is delayed or altogether absent. In terms of their model we could say that it was Goebbels' sinister genius – and perhaps the genius of all successful propagandists – to have recognized these limits in the media and, accordingly, used his spies as a way of compensating for the sense modalities and the orientative feedback his media system lacked. We might, in fact, have reason to suspect that the studies of gatekeepers and opinion leaders may have cast their research too narrowly to grasp the true range of these possibilities.

The next chapter turns to some quite different but related efforts since World War II to form a more systematic conception of information and just such a broader understanding of the role of information in maintaining and in changing social realities.

CHAPTER 6

Instrumental Information

6.1 Morphostatic Information

6.1.1 The Transmission Model of Information

It is only partly true but it is often said that the efforts to design the military and para-military technology of World War II produced as a by-product the first workable concept of information as a measurable and mathematically describable phenomenon. The technologies of radar, automatic gun sights and similar tracking devices, as well as the stabilizers or gyroscopes on naval warships, have all been linked to the development of the formal unit of information since all of them depend upon sensory machinery able to measure and compensate for messages emitted from the environment. Two developments in particular during the immediate post-war period became especially important to the growth of communication research: the information theory of Shannon and Weaver, two telephone engineers working at the Bell Laboratories, and the theory of cybernetics advanced by Norbert Wiener at the Massachusetts Institute of Technology.[1]

Shannon and Weaver produced the first formal transmission model of information. Their model suggested that the successful transmission of information from one place to another depends upon three interrelated criteria: the condition and capacity of the channel through which the communication occurs; the influence of noise from the general environment; and the amount of redundancy in the message itself. Shannon and Weaver steadfastly maintained that their model had no relevancy for human communication, but the model was adapted to the description of human communication nonetheless. Today the concepts of channel capacity, noise, and redundancy have long since lost their original reference to the telephonic phenomena Shannon and Weaver had in mind and are now part of everyday speech; but the concept of redundancy still retains some of the importance Shannon and Weaver attached to it. All naturally occurring languages, for instance, are redundant in their sounds, letters and the combinations thereof. Most languages, in fact, are about fifty percent redundant. Redundancy in communication can be said to promote predictability by establishing continuity with what has preceded it. Redundancy stabilizes information into recognizable formulas and patterns. In a sense it creates order out of variety and maintains it in the face of environmental noise. Information that promotes order and stable patterns is said to have a *morphostatic function.*

In an exchange of information by telephone it is possible to know almost immediately whether and to what extent a message has been understood. The response, of course, is limited to the oral-aural channel, but the process by which the results of a communication return to the source of that communication is similar to the self-corrective feedback identified by Norbert Wiener. Thus, Wiener's notion of feedback adds a fourth factor to Shannon and Weaver's three criteria for the successful transmission of information. Much like redundancy, corrective feedback describes the process through which predictability and pattern are continuously built into the operation of many communication systems.

6.1.2 The Transmission Model of Communication – Schramm

In the 1950s Wilbur Schramm transformed Shannon and Weaver's model into a general model of the human communication process, both direct interpersonal communication and those forms of communication mediated by communication technology. According to Schramm's model, all forms of human communication consist of three interdependent elements – a source, messages, and a destination.[2] Schramm's description became a common-sensical model for representing the relationship between senders and receivers mediated by the use of communication technologies. There was, however, a strategic difference in Schramm's model. Unlike Shannon and Weaver's model of information and interaction through telephonics, the mass communication systems that had become so important a part of Twentieth Century life had little built-in capacity for immediate feedback and no possibility at all for reversing the role of sender and receiver that the telephone accommodated so easily. It was in part because the transmission technologies of mass media systems could not be effectively stabilized by immediate feedback links that some communication theorists initially believed that the role of such information systems should be seen in terms of their capacity for the amplification and acceleration of social change. One to many technologies such as radio and television, sometimes even newspapers, magazines and film, appeared to some to be ideal agents for social change. In other words, what seemed to some to be a destabilizing feature in the information transmission process of mass communication systems (the absence of feedback), appeared to others to indicate the media's potential to accelerate the pace of social change that modernization was beginning to impose upon traditional forms of life everywhere, but most critically in the economically underdeveloped regions of the world.

The difference the transmission model identified between direct interaction (with immediate feedback) and the manner in which some technologies mediated interaction (without immediate feedback) suggested further distinctions. The model suggested there might be important differences between *oral systems* of communication (where most activity depends upon face-to-face relations) and *media systems* (organized around amplification technology with limited capacities for feedback). And it was implied by promoters of the model that media systems could become important sources for the animation and motivation of social change. In this latter case, information was thought to have a *morphogenic function.*

6.2 Morphogenic Information

6.2.1 Communication and Modernization

In a curious way our ideas about the role of media in modernization grew out of a combination of the flow concepts of the last chapter and the information concepts of the present one. By the time mass communication systems began to appear in areas outside of the industrialized northern hemisphere it was generally accepted that the effectiveness of centralized forms of information flow would depend upon mediation at the local level for their influence. Local influence, no matter what the society or culture, were after all personal; and personal influence was a complex and resistant subject matter. Nevertheless, in the heady nationalism that followed the formal decolonization of much of what is now known as the Third World, mass communication was perceived as a symbol if not a means of bringing to these new nations, many of which were divided by tribal, ethnic and regional loyalties, a sense of shared national purpose and direction. The use of communication systems to promote and direct social change, education, collective purpose and identity are morphogenic uses of information.

Views about the morphogenic uses of information are commonly found grouped together with ideas of modernization. The fact that views of information as morphogenic were often connected to concerns for modernization in underdeveloped parts of the world may help explain why the work of the researchers in the previous chapter, concentrated largely on the United States, seems to have received so little attention by the information theorists of the present one.

6.2.2 Development Theory – Lerner, Schramm, McClelland

Of the following theories describing the relationship of mass communication to development, two are wrong and one is only partly correct. In the 1950s Daniel Lerner proposed the most dramatic theory of development. After investigations in parts of the Middle East, Lerner returned to the United States and proposed a general thesis. All development, he suggested, will proceed according to a structural pattern of growth. Somewhat like the lockstep method of education, Lerner listed four stages through which a developing country must pass to reach a developed state: (1) urbanization, (2) literacy, (3) voting, and (4) media participation. As the first stage, urbanization was the key to all the others. Lerner assumed (and for many years it was never questioned) that only after the urban population reached 10% of the total population in a country did the other stages become possible. Literacy, political democracy, and media participation depended upon an urbanizing population base. In retrospect, this was never proved.[3]

A corollary of Lerner's theory, more ingenious and widely accepted in the 1950s, linked personality to the state of societal development. The *physically mobile society,* best typified by Europe and North America, Lerner claimed, had brought about and was in turn dependent upon the *mobile personality,* a personality capable of empathy and, therefore, compatible with the efficient operation of modern society. Two other types, the *traditional personality* and the *transitional personality* were distinguishable by their degree of exposure to mass media. Lerner considered mass media, or rather the information content of the media to be a *mobility multiplier;* and, therefore, it was assumed that the introduction of media provided a necessary and a sufficient condition for creating new values and thus the conditions for changing traditional man into transitional man. Unfortunately, in the decades following the introduction of mass communication into the Third World little evidence was forthcoming to support these early conjectures. Mass media systems might have been a necessary condition for certain new values to gain greater public awareness, but they were not a sufficient condition to guarantee their adoption or acceptance. Contrarily, the possible role of mass media systems in the disintegration of traditional societies, which is not quite the same thing, has not gone unnoticed by the members of such societies.[4]

It was the modifier of the transmission model, Wilbur Schramm, who also modified Lerner's theory. Schramm argued that the Western experience is archetypal or structural, that is, its state of advancement will inevitably occur elsewhere, although under altered circumstances. Because the process of modernization is inevitable, Schramm argued that mass media could rationally assist the process by providing the knowledge necessary for the populace to make rational choices about new behavior and beliefs.[5] The thesis of the West as destiny is, of course, not a new one and it is not an easily refuted thesis either. But critics have noted that Schramm's idea that the availability of knowledge could become the basis for selecting new beliefs and behaviors seems to run counter to most human experience. The availability of knowledge about new beliefs and behaviors might be a *necessary condition* for a rational choice, but what can be observed of human history suggests that knowledge is seldom a sufficient condition for rational choices; nor are beliefs and behaviors themselves necessarily rational outcomes in any case.

Because Lerner and Schramm based themselves more or less exclusively on contemporary and comparative evidence, a British historian, David McClelland, was prompted to examine the history of our own Western industrial development.[6] When McClelland examined a number of newspapers, magazines, and other media forms over time he found that where the content indicated a high concern for achievement, rapid economic development was also likely. His thesis, a much diluted one from that of Lerner and Schramm, suggested only that the mass media have one kind of role amongst many others in creating new norms and values. However, McClelland was able to offer little hard evidence that mass media actually create these new norms and values. Nor was McClelland able to clarify whether changes in attitude and behavior actually precede social development, whether they accompany it, or whether they simply follow along afterward. Mass media systems appear to play some role in social change, but there is little evidence that they can produce by themselves the positive conditions for such changes.

6.2.3 Dependency Theory – A Critique

Many different criticisms have been made of the role of media in modernization, but most critics agree that the belief that information media could amplify and accelerate broad types of social change has had serious flaws. Even if the development of media systems could bring about such profound attitudinal changes, as the theorists of personal influence suggested, these changes come about only if reinforced by local and personal agencies.

Furthermore, while the theories of development promised broad brush strokes of social change, the actual media systems in developing countries often found themselves with the bargain basement information content of the developed world – and with predictably unfortunate results. In Africa, Congolese soldiers stoned Donald Duck on the screen because they felt themselves ridiculed; in the soldiers' experience birds neither talked nor wore uniforms. Similarly, when programs on European farm workers were shown to African villagers they were not believed because the villagers had no prior experience with white men working the land.[7]

Such events were probably more instructive than harmful. More serious by far was the question of whether the dependency of the Third World on the information resources of developed countries might amplify their already substantial economic dependency into a cultural dependency as well.

6.3 Information and Environment – Schwartz

The belief that the media constitute tools for intervention and the belief that information can direct and control social change are both the result of what we might call an *instrumental view* of information, that is, information seen as a tool. In fact, our own long preoccupation with transportation and transmission over vast territories and under difficult conditions resulted in our identifying the "movement of information" so closely with the "process of communication" that they often seem to us to be indistinguishable. We are, advertising specialist Tony Schwartz believes, so captivated by the *transportation analogy* that we sometimes err in thinking that the information in the phone line or in the television signal or in the magazine article is equivalent to a commodity being moved around like any other material product.[8]

But, of course, the flow of information is more than the transmission of information or messages; and the danger in thinking exclusively in terms of the movement of messages from some sender to some destination is that we lose sight of the equally important linkage between information and the human social environment or context into which it flows. If information is treated independently of its environment we may fall into the trap of viewing the recipients of that information as similarly lacking an environment in which the message has meaning for them. As a result we may come to think of the information as the environment; and when we slip into thinking of the information or the message as the total context to which a recipient reacts, we lose sight of the ways in which the environment shapes and refashions the meaning of any message. In mistaking the information for the total environment we can be led to overestimate its potential influence. By overlooking the actual social environment of individuals and groups in the decoding of information we can mistakenly attribute what we see in a message for what others get out of it. This is sometimes known as the "attributive fallacy"; and it is a very dangerous one, not least for social scientists, journalists, and politicians.

Schwartz argues that we must constantly remind ourselves that a state of communication is always present in our environment. But because a state of communication does always exist, understanding information conveyed by the media does not require understanding the message; it requires understanding what the listener-viewer gets out of the experience of the message. Communication is not primarily the result of the information that is directed into an audience; it is primarily the result of what that message draws out of them. Under the influence of the transportation analogy it has sometimes seemed that all we needed for effective communication was clear, unambiguous messages. The argument Tony Schwartz presents, as well as the lessons that have begun to come from the development experiences of the Third World, should caution us that the differences between information and the specific context or environment in which the information is received may be of far greater significance than our transmission models led us to believe. Especially in the Third World, where oral communication systems traditionally have been strong, the efforts to install mass media systems have underscored some consequential ways in which the importance of the oral environment has been overlooked.

6.4 Conclusion

Mass communication systems or amplification systems as they are sometimes called lack direct or immediate forms of feedback. Our now global experience with mass media systems provides us with some tentative warnings about the consequences that the absence of feedback can have: (1) the recipients or users cannot ask for clarification or further related information; (2) recipients or users cannot easily question the information; and (3) distortions arising from information crossing boundaries produced and maintained by culture, social history or group differences cannot be easily controlled. The following chapter looks more closely at how we have begun to redefine the information model to take us more deeply into these social consequences.

CHAPTER 7

Social Information

7.1 Reality Integration

7.1.1 Channel Capacity and Overload

In parts of the "corn belt" it has been noted that if five farmers with shotguns enter a barn full of corn and only four come back out again, the corn-loving but watchful crows stay away. On the other hand, if nine farmers go into the barn and eight come back out again, the crows predictably fly down, believing all is clear. Crows, it would seem, have a boundless taste for corn but a restricted capacity to count gun-toting farmers.

The communication psychologist George Miller has noted that the human brain has seemingly limitless powers of abstraction, but severely limited channel capacity. In a brilliant series of demonstrations in the 1960s Miller was able to show that humans, not unlike crows, have difficulties making judgments of sound, color, and taste when the alternatives go beyond the number seven. Seven, Miller concluded, represents something like a channel capacity, beyond which additional information causes a fall-off in our ability to perform tasks. The concept of information overload, which grows out of Miller's research, we might say identifies for us that point at which more becomes less.[1]

Miller's notion of information input overload puts a new light on Festinger's idea of *cognitive dissonance.* When Festinger's psychologists infiltrated a mystical sect which believed the world would end on a certain date, they were able to observe how, when the date passed and the world didn't, the true believers resolved this difficulty by deciding that a postponement had taken place, thereby allowing them to renew their efforts at the persuasion of others. Similarly, in a few isolated cases among Japanese religious sects the defeat of Japan in World War II for some time was believed to be a fabrication meant to conceal the true state of Japanese victory from the public. In fact, the economic consequences of defeat for the principal losers in World War II, Germany and Japan, have been far more beneficial than the consequences of victory for at least one of the victors, the United Kingdom, all of which could produce "ammunition" for those wishing to sustain such an illusion.

Such extreme responses to crisis-precipitating events are a form of *reality denial,* in which previous versions of reality can be maintained only through breaking in some way with the troubling aspects of the new reality. When information becomes so overwhelming as to necessitate denials of this sort, the result is known as *conceptual dissonance.* And although such cases represent the extreme, less extreme forms of conceptual dissonance commonly result from the difference between our technical capabilities to produce and distribute information on a global scale and our limited individual and group capacities to make sense of it. Precisely because of our limited capacities, some researchers claim that many patterns of social interaction are, in fact, strategies for coping with the complexities of an information-intensive environment.

7.1.2 Social Networks and Social Noise – Klapp

Some communities seem to be able to survive the realities of an information intensive environment better than others. The sociologist Orin Klapp has pointed out that apparently similar information environments will produce dissonance and anxiety in one community while producing consonance and cohesion in another.[2] In San Diego, for instance, neighborhoods comprised of the families of Portuguese Catholic fishermen were found to show few of the symptoms of stress observed in other more heterogeneous neighborhoods nearby. Klapp believes that the difference in ability to cope is strongly influenced by differences in the patterns of social interaction. In Klapp's view when social networks are dense and uniform – stressing reinforcement, redundancy, and coherence – all forms of dissonance are low. This would seem to be the case with the Portuguese fishing families where social networks were characterized by closely knit communities and routines through common work, religion, and family life. Such social networks are characterized by what Klapp calls *nondiscursive feedback*. Nondiscursive feedback consists of all those roles, gestures, body language, and other nonverbal forms of interaction that help to support and stabilize *social feelings*. Conversely, when social networks are less dense and less uniform, there is a greater need for explicit communication and classification. Such behavior is perhaps more typical of bureaucratic settings or schools; these sorts of social networks are more characterized by what Klapp calls *discursive feedback*. Discursive feedback is the basis of most decision-making; we find it wherever people interact primarily through abstraction, classification, qualification, and reasoned argument. According to Klapp, social networks characterized by high degrees of discursive feedback and low degrees of nondiscursive feedback typically experience more frequent and more severe problems of dissonance, both cognitive and conceptual.

Klapp has proposed the term *social noise* to describe this circumstance. A state of social noise can be said to exist when the information input from our social environment exceeds our capacity to form an adequate shared understanding about that input. We experience social noise in several consequential ways: (1) decision lags (difficulty in taking needed decisive action); (2) consensus lags (difficulty in reaching a common agreement); and (3) meaning lags (difficulty in agreeing on purposes and values even when sharing the same factual information). Of the three, meaning lags are perhaps the most significant. Meaning seldom keeps pace with information and meaning depends upon localized networks of people who constitute a sort of social channel capacity.

Formal channels of information such as the mass media are important sources, but they are only indirectly related to our social networks through which information gains its personal meaning. When we come to depend too much upon formal channels, it can result in diminished feedback from our informal social channels and thus in lowered support for and expression of *social feelings.* The consequence may be dissonance and possibly *alienation,* a condition wherein social feelings are replaced by feelings of being a permanent spectator to events and relationships.

Stable social networks seem to depend upon a balancing of formal and informal channels of information, between what Klapp calls (1) *indigenous signals,* which are familiar, nearby, local, communicated in direct personal relationships, immediate, and highly redundant; and (2) *exogenous signals,* which originate outside the community, are wide-ranging, remote in reference, of low redundancy, containing images that cannot be validated by personal interaction, and contribute less to identity.

Some balancing of these informational variables would appear to be essential for social well-being. In the absence of balance, an overloading of exogenous signals may result in social noise; and an overloading of indigenous signals may result in banality. Similarly, too much ritual may discourage learning; and too much learning may produce intolerance for the role of tradition.

An imbalance of information variables produces overload and strategies of reality denial; likewise, a balance of information variables produces reality integration. In Klapp's model reality denial and reality integration are both functions of the informational relationships between the individual and social reality. This way of describing the integrating role of information is functionalistic. When Klapp describes indigenous and exogenous information, he is identifying their function, what they are for and how they are used. In a functionalist sense, all our mass communication systems provide some form of reality integration; direct social relations provide another. Problems, when they do occur for individuals or for social groupings, often are partly the result of some skewing or imbalancing of these distinctive informational forms.

7.2 Organizational Integration

7.2.1 Goals and Purposes

Herbert Simon has suggested that reality integration depends not only upon our balancing of formal channels and social networks, but also upon the role of goals and purposes.[3] When Simon assembled experimental groups and asked them to undertake a variety of cooperative tasks, he was able to observe how they characteristically opted to accomplish these tasks by organizing themselves in highly predictable ways. Simon referred to these uses of informal organizations to accomplish some goal or purpose as *interaction strategies.* For simple tasks like identifying the color of a marble held in common by all members, people commonly adopted a wheel-like arrangement for dealing with one another. In the wheel configuration interaction is organized around a decision-maker at the center. When, however, the task calls for flexibility and even creativity, such as accepting a new idea or changing from task to task an interaction configuration resembling a circle proved to be more practical than the wheel. Efficiency, Simon noted, seems to depend very much upon the character of the individual at the center; flexibility and creativity, in turn, seem to demand a more decentralized structure. Interestingly enough, when Simon tried to impose more complex interaction patterns upon them, the experimental groups reverted toward solutions emphasizing the fewest possible interactions and interpersonal links among themselves. Group pressures, it seems, predictably push us toward simpler interaction networks, at least where some form of work or purposive action or experimentation is involved.

7.2.2 Plans and Editing

The Christie-Luce-Macy experiments in the 1950s provided a primitive sense of the influence of plans upon group interaction.[4] In these experiments groups of participants were asked to discover what color marble was held by all of them in common. Initially, those groups that had been given marbles with solid colors for which there were ordinary names did much better. Groups that received streaked colors for which there are no common names were able to perform at the level of the other groups only when they had invented an adequate vocabulary and negotiated a general acceptance of it. Success in this case depended not only upon organizing an interaction strategy. It depended additionally upon developing a technical vocabulary, or what has been called a plan. Such experiments on task-oriented interaction seem to show our need to coordinate with each other by plans as well as interaction strategies. Plans of this sort resemble blueprints or maps for action by their ability to allow for complexity while maintaining efficiency.

Taken together, plans and interaction strategies underscore the ways we coordinate with others to reduce the complexity of reality through what we might call a form of group editing. Group editing economizes purposive behavior, since at each stage it is the edited information that is communicated. In this way coordinated groups are able to bring about the absorption of uncertainty and uncertainty generated by the complexity of that information could be said to be absorbed through the strategies and organizations themselves.

The interactional strategies, plans, and organizations that Simon identifies bear upon the point made more negatively through Tucker's description of the prisoners' dilemma. In differing ways, Simon and Tucker both suggest that there is a human tendency toward basic forms of coordination and cooperation that arises spontaneously among people faced with similar goals or purposes, even it seems in the face of efforts to inhibit this formation or to impose specific patterns upon it. We can witness this tendency in such simple matters as the passage of people in and out of a crowded doorway or in such complicated dealings as those of international trade. To make the matter a bit clearer, we might say that the tendency toward mutually cooperative strategies and arrangements represents a nearly universal experience, while the specific forms of that experience may depend greatly upon the contexts in which they occur.

7.3 Interactive Feedback

7.3.1 Communication Networks – Rogers and Kincaid

The preceding works stress coordination and cooperation as a defining human tendency. They identify this tendency as an observable human need to draw toward and be drawn toward social relations and organized purposes to which positive values can be assigned and away from those to which negative values are attached or that conflict with established beliefs and behavior. The converging and diverging patterns that result add to a fuller understanding of the social function of feedback and, indirectly, social noise. Simon's experimental subjects, Klapp's Portuguese fishing families, even in a negative way the examples of those imprisoned by circumstances beyond their control, all underscore the significance of interactive feedback in the formation and maintenance of our many interpersonal networks and the values habitually associated with them.

Two communication researchers, Everett Rogers and Lawrence Kincaid, came to a similar appreciation of the importance of these networks when they set out to examine the success of the women of the South Korean village of Oryu Li in organizing community self-sufficiency and generating alternative sources of community wealth.[5] The researchers' experiences in coming to grips with the dynamic character of the communication networks through which these women coordinated their activities convinced them that previous information models had underestimated these interpersonal exchanges through which and in which all forms of information took on their typically convergent and divergent qualities. Contrary to the assumptions associated with the older information models, Rogers and Kincaid suggested that, in their observations of interpersonal networks, *who* exchanges the information often has defining significance over the consequences of *what information* is actually exchanged.

7.3.2 Conclusion

The early models of information – especially those concerned with media persuasion, gatekeeping, and influence – tended to focus their analysis on the transmission of messages rather than upon the social relations involved in this process. The instrumental models of information that followed similarly tended to exaggerate the message content, often to the near exclusion of the complex of social and cultural networks and exchanges in which transmitted information found both its meaning and its purpose. In retrospect, the failure of these models to acknowledge the significance of the interpersonal and social context of information flows can be traced to the models' failure to take seriously the diverse networks of human relations underlying their abstract and largely quantitative plottings of the flow of information itself. By contrast, the experiments and the field observation studies of this chapter emphasize the importance, not of messages, but of exchange relations maintained through interactive feedback. The unit of analysis toward which such studies seem to be moving is one that begins, not with the isolated messages, but with the dynamic patterns of interpersonal organization.

Taken together, these revised ideas on how information is processed, psychologically and socially, provide a tentative conception of the informational relationships connecting our personal and social realities. In a cautious way we could also read these revisions as a reminder that our theoretical model building over the past few decades in practice has been something akin to a channel capacity, defining and limiting what is to be given emphasis – and constraining our insight accordingly.

CHAPTER 8

Information and Codification

8.1 Codification – Bateson

8.1.1 Metacommunication

It is occasionally noted that school children repeat the games and rhymes of past generations, even though such games are little more than a vague and distant memory to their parents. The repetition of such games should remind us just how subtly our own identity and that of our social world as well depends upon the redundancy of themes for its continuity. It is perhaps the primary role of information to create redundancy out of variety and, in such manner, to fashion the patterns and predictability of our relations to others as well as to the social order. Rhymes are simply an example of this process. Rhymes help to socialize us into childhood and they remain there performing their socializing function when we ourselves move on.

This example can help us appreciate the role of codes. In everyday occurrence much coding is *situation defining;* that is, it simply establishes what type of interaction is going on, such as childhood play. Bateson calls this process of defining the situation a *metacommunicative function*; and he invented a simple description for metacommunication. Every form of communication according to Bateson contains two sorts of meaning: "On the one hand, the message is a statement or report about events at a previous moment, and on the other hand it is a command – a cause or stimulus for events at a later moment."[1] *Report and command,* thus, refer to the way in which communication contains not only an *information content,* but in addition one or several *metacommunicative propositions.* These metacommunicative propositions tell us about the limits that the communicators of a message wish to see placed on the meaning of that message (play, for instance). In a broader sense the role of metacommunication tells us how the communicator sees or wishes to see his/her relationship to others. Bateson insists that all forms of communication contain positional information of this sort; and feedback, he insists, serves primarily a positional function. But what is perhaps most important is to see how significantly our everday reality is defined and constrained by the information feedback we receive through a variety of metacommunicative codes.

8.1.2 The Schizophrenic Switchboard Operator

When Bateson first described his ideas about metacommunicative codes to his friend Norbert Wiener, Wiener typically suggested that they construct a mechanical example to demonstrate concretely what he meant. When later the two men emerged from Wiener's workshop, they had indeed produced a machine of sorts, but one which was *incapable* of distinguishing between code and the normal information content of communication. Breakdowns and failures, the two scientists pointed out, are sometimes useful moments for disclosing how things normally work. The machine they produced was supposed to act something like a mildly schizophrenic switchboard and it worked (or didn't work) something like this. If you wished to place a phone call, imagining yourself in a hotel for a convention, you would normally pick up the room phone receiver and give the switchboard operator the number of the party you wanted. Let's say you wished to speak to somebody at number 256. The operator would then connect your number with number 256 through the switchboard and, when your party came on the line, communication could commence. However, in Bateson's and Wiener's design the operator stayed on the line and, if in the course of the conversation one party mentioned another three digit number, perhaps by way of a proposal to meet for drinks downstairs at 5:30, the operator would immediately break into the connection and reconnect the party supplying this new information to number 530. By virtue of its inability to distinguish between numerical information and the different contexts in which it was used, Bateson's and Wiener's design recalls how fundamentally important it is to be able to distinguish information content from various sorts of propositional statements – what Bateson calls the metacommunicative code. Or, as Bateson might say it, the switchboard operator was unable to make the distinction consistently between one sort of situation defining information and the rest; all information that appeared situation defining was treated as if it were so.

Although the design never made it as far as the patent office, its failure helps to demonstrate the importance of codes for successful interaction. By its failure the schizophrenic switchboard helps demonstrate what might happen if we had to do without shared codes. It also demonstrates how, in our normal dealings with others, our many social and cultural codes unconsciously and automatically define and constrain our relationship to others. Schizophrenics, it is worth noting, seem to have a great deal of trouble with metacommunicative codes. Many of the schizophrenics with whom Bateson worked as a therapist were preoccupied with situation defining questions. Not unlike the switchboard operator of Bateson's design, they tended to key on matters that the rest of us would seldom take note of; often, Bateson noted, these preoccupations became immobilizing for them. Bateson has hypothesized that the communication of schizophrenics may systematically differ from that of the rest of us in terms of the *conscious* attention given to situation defining information, while in other respects appearing much the same.[2]

Few of us are as sensitive or as vulnerable as schizophrenics to the way codes define and constrain our relationships with others, but most of us have had momentary experiences when our defining sense of reality is disturbed or brought into question. One classic example is the experience of group hypnosis. For centuries travellers to the markets and bazaars of the Indian subcontinent have witnessed the so-called rope trick. There before their disbelieving eyes, a local charmer suspends a rope in midair and then in full view of the surrounding crowd the man of magic carefully climbs up the rope, suspending himself literally on thin air. Witnesses to such feats are, of course, charmed; but those with the presence of mind to take a photograph or two later find themselves with nothing more unusual than the pictures of an Indian citizen calmly standing rope in hand in the middle of an appreciative crowd. Hypnosis in its many forms, entertaining and therapeutic, is an elegant demonstration that reality may be more negotiable than we thought. In our everyday lives, what we sometimes have trouble recognizing is the extent to which we treat our reality as nonnegotiable precisely because of our unquestioned acceptance of the codes that habitually define and constrain it.

8.2 Interactional Codes – Watzlawick

8.2.1 Symmetrical and Complementary Codes

It is difficult and surprising for us to discover the extent to which our habitual pattersn of interaction can be described in terms of codes. From his therapeutic studies, Paul Watzlawick has identified two interactional codes, which he calls symmetrical and complementary and which he believes are nearly universally present in our culture.[3] Complementary codes tend to maximize the differences between parties. Especially in close interpersonal relationships, we often find that behavior characterized by dominance, authority, and primacy in one partner is paired with behavior characterized by dependency, obedience, and subservience in the other. These role-relationships, Watzlawick says, are more than coincidental; they are both functional (mother-child, teacher-student, manager-worker, officer-soldier) and interlocking (each role is complementary to and doesn't exist without the other). In other words, the patterns are situation defining. By contrast, *symmetrical codes* tend to minimize the differences between parties. Relationships based on symmetrical codes are characterized by the tendency of each side to mirror the behavior of the other (boasting, flattering, quarreling, and all forms of competition). In each case, of course, there can be many different degrees of difference and similarity; but it is the types of behavior that are to be emphasized. Watzlawick's two types of interaction involve high degrees of repetition and redundancy but it is assumed that they function in a way that maintains overall stability or balance in a relationship. When complementarity produces inflexibility (for instance, in the need of children to transcend the mother-child pattern as they mature), or when symmetry generates escalation (in quarreling that turns into violence, for instance, or competition that transcends the normal rules or conventions), either type of interaction can lead to its own forms of crisis, or pathology.

The point Watzlawick makes about the codified information contained in our interaction patterns is sometimes a difficult one for us to accept. Most of our interactions fall into redundant forms that make us predictable if not always reassuring in our relationships with others. Symmetry and complementarity are just two examples of these largely unconscious patterns within which our personal relationships are fashioned. But, if it is difficult for us to accept the patterned and predictable nature of interaction that Watzlawick describes, even more disturbing things have been proposed about how linguistic codes define and locate us within the larger social order.

8.3 Linguistic Codes – Bernstein

8.3.1 Restricted and Elaborated

Basil Bernstein first identified the verbal dimension of codes, or what is called *linguistic coding.*[4] In his studies of various social groups in England, Bernstein discovered that different forms of social relationship may generate quite different systems of speech; and because a speech system is closely tied to our social relationships and through them to social structures, it appears that different social structures may bring about different systems of speech, what Bernstein calls different linguistic codes.

Bernstein distinguished two basic linguistic codes which he called elaborated and restricted. *Elaborated codes* facilitate verbal expression and individual description; they typically involve grammatically complex sentence structures, the use of prepositions to indicate logical relationships, or to indicate temporal and spatial contiguity, as well as explicit individual qualifications on matters, and the use of a complex conceptual hierarchy for the organization of experience. By contrast, *restricted codes* do not facilitate individual expression; they typically involve short simple sentences of generally poor construction, the frequent use of short commands and questions, limited use of adjectives and adverbs in favor of traditional idioms, and the use of factual statements as both reason and conclusion.

Bernstein's codes can be thought of as indicating the degree of openness or closedness in the particular social structure where the linguistic code is found. For instance, restricted codes can be observed in such closed communities as prisons, the armed services, and criminal subcultures. Elaborated codes on the other hand are readily observed in organizations stressing verbal initiative, corporations, bureaucracies, including of course much of the system of schooling. In the latter case, Bernstein's work with school children suggests that linguistic codes may help to explain the relative backwardness of some working class children in school. Elaborated codes and schooling, Bernstein feels, are both strongly tied to the needs and the reality of the middle class. Codes establish a child's social identity from his or her earliest family and community experiences; and these social relationships regulate the linguistic code which constitutes the personal reality of the child. The child takes his linguistic code to school, to play, and brings it back home again. In time some children may be able to modify it; some become adept at using other codes. The working class child, for instance, may come to feel comfortable with the elaborated codes favored by the middle class. Then again, this may not happen; and even if it does happen, a lengthy and painful period of transition may be required to gain the necessary competency. But, whatever the case, it is Bernstein's point that a child's personal and social reality will be fashioned and reinforced for himself and for others every time the child speaks.

8.3.2 Language and Class

One problem encountered with the concept of codes is that they appear to be more fixed and permanent than is actually the case. Perhaps we could say that the role of codes remains constant, while the content of particular codes and their relative influence upon us does not. Thus, when we find ourselves negotiating our way from one set of social roles to another we may also find ourselves limited in these negotiations by the codes available to us, and sometimes discouraged by the personal and social costs that may be involved in the pursuit of alternatives.

This last matter is a crucial one because it involves the relationship of class, status, and language. The child who adopts the elaborated code of the school sometimes learns quickly the difficulties created by placing himself or herself at odds with the restricted codes of family or childhood friends. Until recently not much had been done to help us understand how communication in general and language in particular relates to matters of class. However, if the question of communication and class has been neglected until recently, the question of the relation of communication to language has been one of the most important themes in this century. In the last few chapters the issues of language and other symbolic modes of communication have been respectfully avoided. In the next few chapters, the role of language and symbol in the production of reality becomes central – and a necessary preamble to a further discussion of codes.

PART THREE

Intersubjectivity — Modes of Symbolic Interaction

Although rich in insights, the emphasis on empirical enclosures has disturbed some researchers because of the way it seems to neglect the full range of symbols and language in communication. We can appreciate the ways in which social roles and social circumstances are defined and regulated through information and codification; and we can grasp the importance of the strategies through which we try to reduce the uncertainty in a variety of *immediately given situations.* However, when we ask how it is that we are also able to transcend the immediacy of things and of our own actions to deal with other times, places, memories, and projections, actual or imaginary, that also make up our reality, we need to be able to conceive of communication as primarily a symbolic experience. In the chapters to follow the question of how communication functions to allow us to get beyond the immediacy of our environment is explored through examining how our languages, story systems, and a variety of institutions work to continuously construct and modify the linguistic-symbolic relationship between ourselves and our social reality.

CHAPTER 9

Language

9.1 Verbal Forms

9.1.1 Introduction

When we associate the use of language principally with the transmission of information, we can lose sight of its other capacities, especially the *capacity for speculation* and the *capacity to date.* The capacity for speculation permits us to consider alternatives to the facts as they appear to us. The capacity to date occurrences allows us a specialized form of memory, and thereby provides us with a record of our own personal past and our historical past. The creation of new meanings as well as the changes in meaning over time and place are additional matters that result from the capacity of language to define and constrain reality.

These capacities of language are second nature to us. They can be sensed first hand whenever we have the experience of moving between countries or even between cultures sharing the same language but separated by tradition and different paths of development. George Bernard Shaw, tongue in cheek, referred to these linguistic bonds when he described the United States and the United Kingdom as one people separated by a common language.

Whether we see language as defining and constraining reality — or, as we could also describe it, as generating and preserving meaning – its role in human culture is nearly universal. There are no known cultures without spoken language and all cultures use language to construct stories or narratives through which in part their culture is reproduced. The nearly universal role of language in human culture is thought to rest upon two features: one, that we all have the ability to learn a language (innate feature); and two, that all languages have rules of combination, or grammaticality (structural feature). For the moment, at least, it is the structural feature of language that we know most about.

9.1.2 Aphasia

The linguist Roman Jakobson has noted that people display a narrower ability as senders of verbal messages and a wider ability as receivers of them.[1] Since perception always involves categorization it would seem that our capacity for categorizing what we perceive usually outdistances our capacity for expressing it. When the sender speaks he is collapsing many levels of language into a single one. Contrarily, a receiver, when taking in a verbal message, has far more levels of language at his disposal. In a broader sense our cognitions, or thought processes, can continue to gain complexity from their ongoing social character, but our verbal performances remain severely restricted by our individual competence in the act of speaking.

People suffering from a type of brain damage known as aphasia lose much of this latter capacity to express ideas. Specifically, aphasics, as they are called, lose the ability to express themselves with regard to situations that do not actually exist, such as situations past and future and those situations otherwise not immediately at hand. This loss of the power to project and to speculate makes the aphasic virtually helpless to deal with anything beyond the immediate. In a rather cruel way the plight of aphasics emphasizes the generative role of language we normally take for granted, what linguistics commonly refer to as its features of *production* and *displacement.*

9.1.3 Language as Production

Speech sounds differ from all others. They are better identified by the right ear, while all other acoustics such as music and noise are more easily processed by the left ear. Speech sounds result from a limited number of *distinctive features* attached to each language. Through studying the development of language in children linguists have been able to identify these distinctive features for each language and to describe precisely their rules of internal combination and arrangement (phonological rules). The number of such distinctive features and rules of combination in any language is very limited. Their role is to govern the admissibility and interconnection of the various elements of a language, and are commonly referred to as the *invariant principles* of a given language. The role of invariants in language may be analogous to the self-regulating and self-steering function of a feedback process.

At the same time that the sound patterns of a language have invariants, there also exists a set of invariants at the point where phonemes combine into words, and words into sentences. Here the relation between the words themselves is governed by another set of invariants, called morphemes, which most of us know something about through learning the grammatical rules by which words must be related to one another. By means of the interplay of sounds and contexts, and words and contexts, the invariants of language interact with the requirements of specific speech situations to bring about the production and creation of linguistic expression.

The meaning that words have depends upon the combination of *grammatical meaning* (what kind of word – noun, verb, adjective, preposition, etc.) and *lexical meaning* (the general things a word represents – objects, relations, ideas, etc.). Lexical meaning is also both invariant (defined in the dictionary sense) and responsive to the way in which the different contexts in which it is used result in new meanings through modifications of the old ones. Thus it is that through mastering a finite number of phonemes and grammatical rules we gain the capacity to combine and recombine words into an infinite stream of sentences and meanings.[2]

9.1.4 Language as Displacement

An infant first encounters speech through the talk of those around him. As his awareness increases, the child internalizes the speech he hears. The development of inner speech, a development which is impaired in verbal disorders such as that of aphasia, permits the child to gradually free himself from the immediacy of the environment. In the acquisition of language the emergence of the subject-predicate sentence is believed to be a vital feature in this process, providing children with the linguistic means to escape from their own surroundings and to begin to consider discontinuous events, those separated from them by time and space, as well as other events purely fictitious and imaginary.

The concept of displacement thus indicates how it is that we can produce complicated acts of thought and speech when no actual stimulus from such events is present. Taken together, production and displacement describe universal features of language by which we are able to form and to modify our symbolic realities. When the invariant features of language production combine with the variety of actual and displaced contexts to which language can refer we have an indication of both the *stabilizing* and the *dynamic* features of a language system.

9.2 Constitutive Speech Forms

9.2.1 Speech Acts – Searle

A speech act, according to John Searle, involves a speaker, a hearer, and an utterance. Typically when we speak, we do so by following rules or conventions.[3] Searle likens the rules of speaking to the rules of a game. Football depends upon acting in accordance with agreed rules, and we could say that without these rules – or without some similar rules – there would be no such activity. The rules of football make possible the very activity that the rules exist to regulate. Rules of this sort that make possible and regulate behavior are called *constitutive rules.* Successful speech acts depend upon similar sorts of constitutive rules.

This somewhat circular description of constitutive rules led Searle to conclude that every speech act between a speaker and a hearer contains two distinct (but not necessarily separate) parts:

one containing the content of the speech act and another containing an indication from the speaker as to how the content of his remarks is to be taken. This latter function-indicating device, as Searle calls it, resembles Bateson's concept of metacommunication; both identify the speaker's attempt to signal how the hearer ought to relate to what is said. Word order, stress, intonation, punctuation, and such constructions as "I warn," "I demand," and "I promise" would all be function-indicating devices. In many actual speech situations the context itself will often be sufficient to make clear how the message is to be taken. Thus, speech acts do not describe so much the content of communication as the conventional ways in which the speaker anticipates and shapes the hearer's response. In the performance of a speech act the words we utter *have meaning* and can also be said to *mean something* on the part of the speaker. This difference allows us to grasp the relationship between what Searle calls the *intentional aspect* of speech (the desire to produce an effect) and the *conventional aspect* of speech (the role of the rules of expression in the production of that effect). Both intentional and conventional aspects of the speech act constitute ways by which we attempt to manage and stabilize the effects of language in our dealings with others.

9.2.2 Social Speech Acts

When we see language as merely a set of rules or even conventions of interaction we can miss its role in the creation of social relationships. The process through which we develop as individuals while also evolving into a variety of roles in society is also dependent upon the *constitutive rules* of speaking a language.

In our language-based social order even the deaf are subject to this constraint. As more than one observer has noted, the deaf are assigned roles by virtue of their handicap and many come to accept these roles as "natural" for them.

Ethnographers of communication, who study actual acts of speaking and hearing, stress the importance of the *differences* among communicators within society. Communicators in actual fact are characterized by the different roles they play in the social order, by differential abilities as senders and receivers, and by differential skills and opportunities in using the various codes and channels of communication available. Additionally, differences can be observed between societies. "Peoples," Dell Hymes says, "do not all, everywhere, use language to the same degree, in the same situations, or for the same situations, or for the same things; some peoples focus upon language more than others."[4]

Different rates of social and intellectual development make for complex forms of inequality in society. Taken together with differential roles, abilities, and opportunities, they all draw attention to the many ways in which social relationships and social situations shape selectively *what is said* in society, by whom and to whom. When we consider the speech act in light of these additional variables affecting the hearer or the receiver, it can be seen how easily the use of modern media, which normally do not take these differences into account in preparing their own sorts of communicative acts, can and do complicate the matter of *what can be said.*

9.3 Presentational Forms

Susanne Langer has pointed out that language is not the only device for conveying information and meaning. Music, art, myth, and ritual all create situations of meaning; and, like speech acts, these nonverbal forms of presentation depend upon similar rules and conventions. *Presentational forms* such as ritual and myth exhibit similar powers of production and displacement. Through rules and conventions art and music express an infinite variety of combinations, allowing us to pass beyond the immediate and bring things, actual or fictive, before our minds. By their use in new situations, new combinations produce new meanings and even new conventions.[5]

Through presentational forms, linguistic and nonlinguistic, we actively shape our own realities. Our capacities of anticipation and mutual role-taking assist this process by allowing us to assess the possible effect of our actions; and the social situations we find ourselves bound up in also actively shape what is said. Much more needs to be said about the role of presentational forms in the construction of our social-symbolic reality. The following chapter explores one of the most basic presentational forms, our use of stories.

CHAPTER 10

Story Systems

10.1 Stories and Frames

10.1.1 Story Forms

Stories, it has been suggested, are perhaps our principal cultural artifact. All cultures and societies use stories as a means of transcending the immediacy of things and of experience. Stories are a part of the process by which the power of displacement of language extends our awareness across time and space. Through stories we are able to have events brought before our minds. Distant happenings reach us through stories, as do recountings of the miraculous and the unusual. Equally, stories provide us with a link to the past: the therapist who asks his client to recall past experiences which may illustrate problems in the present, or the efforts of the defense and the prosecution to establish guilt or innocence by soliciting testimony from witnesses to prior events, are all examples of the use of narrative devices.

Stories, of course, involve more than the recounting of events from other times and places. Since they constitute a nearly universal form for the organization and dissemination of experience, they are an important means for creating social meaning and a shared sense of participation in both a common culture and a particular social order. Stories may arise from a single context, but invariably will be encountered through quite different ones. If stories and storytellers abstract from the events they describe, audiences reverse this process by adding to them. All of which suggests that the production and presentation of stories are richly and complexly related to the ways in which we interact with them.

10.1.2 The Psychological Frame – Bateson

The frames we commonly find around pictures, Gregory Bateson claims, are "an instruction to the viewer that he should not extend the premises which obtain between the figures within the picture to the wall paper behind it."[1] In a sense the picture frame is external evidence for a psychological process by which we limit and edit our experience of the world. Through framing devices we come to be able to make sense out of each other's utterances and those objects and events that reach us through the complex array of special channels and forms of communication. The relationship of a frame to what is contained within the frame (the report, or the content) may be analogous to the relationship between a map and the territory it describes. Several psychological studies have observed that people not only consult maps, they actively construct them and use them as cognitive guides for their own actions. Frames and maps, Bateson believes, resemble premises about how things are. As communicators they provide us with a basis for understanding the reports and messages contained within the frames through which we encounter reality. The psychological frame is thus a metacommunicative feature. Somewhat like the invariants of language, the frame limits the *selective abstraction* and *selective representation* of information and experience. And because frames guide both the presentation of meaning to others and the interpretations we make of what we receive, the frame is an important basis for understanding just what it is that we do when we try to take the point of view of others. Frames rather than contents constitute the basis of our shared or intersubjective experience.

10.1.3 The Theatrical Frame – Goffman

Goffman used Bateson's notion of frame to describe how "staged interaction" is presented and audienced.[2] In the case of plays, radio drama, and novels, he found that writers, producers, and performers all recognize and use frames as a conventional means by which audiences or readers can enter into the fictive world presented. The ability to transform one kind of experience into another – for the writer and performer to transform everyday reality into a fictive one or for audiences to transform their everyday reality into an unreal one for a period of time and just as easily to transform it back again – depends upon commonly shared *framing conventions.*

Within each form of staged interaction Goffman identified several different frames based upon what he called *states of information.* States of information describe, for instance, the playwright's control of awareness, both that of the characters and the audience. A playwright can choose to have the audience be *less informed* about an important fact than the characters in the play, *equally informed,* or *more informed.* Suspense frequently takes the first form, drama or romance the second, and comedy the third. Even in the latter case, however, control remains with the playwright, Goffman notes, because "in the very degree that the focus shifts from what the audience is to discover to what a character is to discover, the audience must be kept in ignorance of the *response* of the character to that eventual discovery."[3]

Film draws upon similar framing conventions with the additional feature that the director can direct attention to the nuances of gesture and expression by varying the camera angle and distance. Both of these forms approximate the "multiple-channel effect," the fact that events tend to present themselves to us through several channels. We apprehend events by shifting attention from one channel to another and by using our eyes to reconfirm what we hear, feel, and smell. Goffman calls this *quick framing,* and because radio audiences, for instance, only *hear* what is presented, this single channel must provide functional equivalents. Such devices are familiar to most radio audiences: volume control to simulate distance, music as a scene-changing device, fade-ins for country, city, or other specifically locational sounds which appear normally at the beginning of a scene and fade-out before talk occurs. The contrast with actual experience can be noted in scenes involving such events as the opening of locks, where during the interval of "lock turning" sounds, the voices will not be heard. Stage and screen actors, when working in radio, find that they have to learn these conventions as part of the pacing required for their roles.

In contrast to both plays and radio drama, the novel grants special license to the writer. Unlike the playwright who has to speak through his characters and the radio scriptwriter who depends upon the aural channel exclusively, the writer of novels can shift points of view as he wishes, including excursions into the past or projections into the future. He can draw upon greater resources of information to describe the actions and motives of his characters. And because the novel is not limited in any sense to the "real time" of theatre or radio, the writer is limited only by the conventions of length that may be dictated by publishers.

These forms of staged interaction suggest that specialized story systems differ from ordinary interaction in the way they control both the *orientation* and the *information states* of the audience. The theatrical frame directs our attention through a series of conventions which, while they resemble the way we frame our actual experience, could be said to differ in the degree of *presentational control.*

10.2 The News Frame – Tuchman

Gaye Tuchman found a similar use of framing conventions in the organization of news, both in newspapers and in television newscasting. "The news frame," she concluded, "organizes everyday reality and the news frame is part and parcel of everyday reality."[4] While this statement may seem almost circular in its logic, Tuchman wants us to see the way in which newsmaking is a form of constructing reality as well as simply presenting it. Frames that arise out of past experience impose an order on present reality. Frames place boundaries on our perception of reality; and, thus, they guide the transformation of occurrences into events, whether "fictive" events or "news" events. In newsmaking (the construction of news events), frames are part of the formal narratives that newspapers conventionally employ. These narrative modes through which events are communicated to readers also define and constrain the newsgathering process. How a story will be presented to the readers acts as a kind of "method" for "guiding" reporters to the "appropriate facts" for its telling. The conventional structure of story telling in newspapers, thus, partly determines what facts reporters find to tell.

Reporters, we might say, are guided to the facts by the questions they habitually ask; and the questions they habitually ask are influenced by the form of presentation they habitually follow to tell their stories. The way in which a news frame is at one and the same time both a response to a new occurrence and itself the result of previous transformations of occurrences into stories is referred to as its *reflexiveness.* News, consequently, is also a product of the methods for gathering and presenting it. By contrast, when historians, sociologists, and others examine old newspapers for evidence of past times, they are dealing with what is called the *indexical* aspects of the past; they do not always take account of the conventions through which newspapers habitually create facts through the news frame. Using newspapers as sources for the historical record, let alone the present, can be fraught with dangers if we fail to respect the reflexive aspects of the production and presentation of the news. When we draw upon such data without taking account of the context of production, Tuchman warns us, we may be mistaking the matters reported for the historical condition itself.[5]

These two features of news construction, the reflexive and the indexical, are considered by ethnomethodologists like Goffman and Tuchman to be *invariants* of the process of professional story-telling. We tend to ignore the extent to which news is story telling, or to acknowledge it only through feelings of uneasiness about how something we have seen or heard has been presented to us. The production and presentation of stories, especially through such formal channels as film, radio, television, and most newspapers, depend upon a third invariant feature – the *documentary method* of interpretation. The documentary method of presenting materials is so commonplace that it is difficult for us to grasp that it is also a device for interpretation. What we experience through modern forms of media comes to us already framed and edited. And although we may have great latitude in our capacity to read meaning into what we encounter through these channels, the investigations of Bateson, Goffman, and Tuchman suggest that the special frames and methods of editing which help to establish the nonfictional status of the stories we see, hear, and read create this status in part through these devices of presentation themselves. The documentary form of story telling seems to have acquired a special status among our many forms of presentation. This helps explain why so many media critics and media practitioners continue to stress the vulnerability to manipulation in all those forms of expression which, like the news frame, are *conventionally* associated with the presentation of facts. In the twentieth century, the tradition to which such factitious forms of story telling belong is frequently referred to as realism. Or, if we wish to be more accurate about the presentational factors involved, we might call it *documentary realism.*

10.3 The Dramatistic Process – Burke

"However important to us is the tiny sliver of reality each of us has experienced first-hand," Kenneth Burke has commented, "the whole overall 'picture' is but a construct of our symbol-systems."[6] Although most of us develop a mature ability to use symbols, in our everyday experience we seldom see the central role of frames and symbols in the production and presentation of our reality. Burke labels as *naive verbal realism* the commonly held notion that reality comes to us through our sense organs unmediated and unconstructed.

Like the others cited in this chapter, Burke sees the use of language and communication to convey information as only a *secondary function.* Primarily, language and communication serve as a form of *action* through which the everyday world is symbolically constructed. Dramatism is Burke's way of referring to the fact that the forms of meaning in our social world – whether those that come to us as scientific facts, as news and information, or as entertainment – come to us through *symbolic forms of presentation.* As students of communication Burke draws our attention to the importance of the forms behind the creation of symbolic action. For every action there must be an agent; there must be a scene in which the agent acts, and to act the agent must employ some means or agency. And for all this to happen there must be a purpose. Act, scene, agent, agency and purpose constitute Burke's *dramatistic pentad.* For every symbolic action, the pentad constitutes the minimal complexity involved.[7]

It is possible to think of Burke's pentad, which he also calls *the act frame,* as an extention of Searle's speech act (speaker, hearer, utterance) to include the dramatistic elements underlying the symbolic nature of the interaction. As Goffman noted, authors and performers acknowledge these elements in a formal way as part of staged interaction. And as we have seen, the types of presentation encountered through the news media are even more formal and explicit efforts to manage the meaning of events. When newsmakers employ the documentary method of story telling, they do so in order to limit the sorts of meaning an audience can get out of the event described. The news frame is thus a striking example of how events are fashioned into those restricted symbolic acts called information.

10.4 Conclusion

This discussion of story systems is meant to draw our attention to the productive and performative features underlying all symbol-systems. Much symbolic meaning comes to us in the form of staged interaction, whether through fictive devices or documentary ones. By disclosing the presence of such devices in the presentation of events, we become more knowledgeable about the conventions underlying the construction and dissemination of our symbolic reality.

CHAPTER 11

Symbols and Symbolization

11.1 The Diffusion and Integration of Symbols

11.1.1 Introduction

In modern society stories to be told must be systematically organized, adapted, reproduced, and disseminated, all of which requires a complex arrangement of professional and skilled labor. This reproduction and dissemination process is continuously carried out through a variety of modes and institutions. The role of such modes and institutions in the diffusion and integration of social reality is conspicuous and central. They help to shape and maintain the norms, values, and belief structures we share as part of our common culture; and they do so through the efficacious use of words, symbols, and rituals. This chapter is a tentative sketch of these modes and institutions in the integration of our symbolic reality.

11.1.2 Symbols as Labels

The power of symbols is the power to name reality. Institutions have a disproportionate share of this power. This is especially true of social institutions, such as the family, government, economic institutions, defense, and education, as well as such institutionalized practices as manners, etiquette, entertainment, health, welfare, religion, art, science, and technology. The sociologist Hugh Duncan observed that what distinguishes an institution's use of symbols from individual usage is the vastly greater capacity of institutions to label experience and to name reality. "A name," Duncan said, "is a *goad* to action, not simply a thought *about* action."[1] Names not only describe the social order but also prescribe many of the roles to be played out in these names. It is not simply imagistic to say that much has happened in the name of the cross or in the name of communism, capitalism or democracy. Naming is labelling; and the social act of labelling carries potentials, for victimage as well as higher purpose. The witch hunts of the seventeenth century in Europe and America, or in our own century the political witchhunting for communists in the United States or for revisionists in countries under the Soviet sphere of influence are all consequences of the power to label. Propaganda, another example of this power to name and to label, is a systematic combination of story systems with the diffusion capacity of mass communication. And because propagandists have made such deliberate use of modern mass media, propaganda is often thought of as a legacy of twentieth century institutions.

11.1.3 The Role of Dominant Symbols

Some symbols are more significant than others. Dominant symbols are often those associated with our political and religious life and with their various institutional practices. In the manifestation and maintenance of power in society, symbols like myths are related to public needs for reassurance and order. "Every symbol," the political analyst Murray Edelman says, "stands for something other than itself, and it also evokes an attitude, a set of impressions, or a pattern of events associated through time, through space, through logic, or through imagination with the symbol."[2] There are, he believes, essentially two types of political symbols, *referential symbols* and *condensation symbols.*[3] Referential symbols are those which provide an economical means of referring to the objective elements in a larger situation, especially elements that can be identified in the same way by different people. Highway death tolls are one such example, specifically those that are routinely announced with ritualistic solemnity during the course of a holiday weekend. Such symbols have significant emotional impact, although their impact upon popular conceptions of the danger of driving or the importance of safety are unclear. Interestingly, the death toll statistics for "long weekends" are marginally higher than the average death toll for a normal three day period over a weekend. Hence, one could make a case for the effectiveness of referential symbols on behavior; but given the much higher volume of traffic and other activities during holiday weekends, one could also make the case that such periods are significantly *safer* and *less dangerous* than so-called normal weekends.

Condensation symbols are those which evoke the emotions associated with the situation, especially feelings of patriotism, anxiety, or reverence. Condensation symbols are not attached to the immediate environment, but play upon the capacity of language for displacement. In their more sinister forms, condensation symbols can create and maintain political fantasies about witches, reds, dupes, spies, foreigners, agitators and so on. In retrospect, the orchestrated efforts to make the "Jew" and the "communist" into a condensation symbol evoking the fears, anxieties, and hostilities of ordinary Germans during the Nazi era are a lingering reminder of the force and the bitter consequences within our own recent history.

In the formation of public opinion, symbols can serve as a form of reality checking, for instance in the use of statistics or other information on food stuffs, automobile safety or efficiency, economic conditions, and so on. Most referential symbols provide us with a means for *reality checking,* for an objective appraisal of our immediate conditions. On the other hand, symbols also serve to promote the formation of opinion where no reality check is possible. In these instances symbols function to promote social adjustment or to project inner tensions onto some symbolic entity. Remote political events in distant parts of the globe have frequently served such ends. Especially for the media-informed and media-dependent public, remote political events can be turned into condensation symbols, emotional in impact, calling for conformity at home and acting as a focus for psychological tensions.

Within our own immediate past, the close identification of "oil" with a variety of fears, anxieties, and hostilities provides an ongoing example of a symbol with both referential forms of reality checking (high prices, gasoline efficient or inefficient cars) and condensational forms with few opportunities for reality checking (oil prices as a scapegoat for the problems of inflation, the Arabs as the source of one's own economic problems or anxieties about the future, even the oil companies as rallying points for reforms such as self-sufficiency). Condensation symbols assist in the formation of opinion in periods of crisis or of *dètente*, but they may occasionally do so in the absence of realistic details; and occasionally they may do so by willful and purposive manipulation. Thus, when broadcasters sometimes try to explain away the complexities of their own difficult role in this process by saying they simply give the public what it wants to hear, they may be saying in a cynical way that what the public appears to want is not news but symbols.

Much that we can learn about the power of dominant symbols can help to identify ways in which professional communicators and communication researchers might better recognize and respond to these potentials of symbols. The condition of remoteness, for example, would seem to have profound influences upon symbolic meaning. *Distant political events* seem to be more powerful sources for manipulative symbols than events closer to our immediate context or events which we can cross-check with our own personal or interpersonal experiences. Likewise, *psychological distance* from symbols seems to evoke perceptions that heighten emotional impact rather than reducing it. *Symbol acts,* it has been suggested, refer to those communications which have symbols as their exclusive objects, and which, because they refer only to other symbols, either lack reality-checking referents or function in ways that obscure them.[4]

11.2 The Regulation of Symbolization

11.2.1 Introduction

To understand how symbolic meaning is formed, diffused, and integrated into reality, and how it is that people can be both passified and aroused by their public communication, we need a sense of the *expressive form* of symbolization, what is sometimes called *ritual.* Political and religious institutions are particularly effective in evoking and reinforcing particular responses in their publics. Although this is more readily evident in organized religion, political rituals can be seen in such repeated activities as legislative debates, courtroom proceedings, public announcements of foreign and domestic policies, and, increasingly in our own day, in the use of the news conference for a variety of official and semi-official purposes. All convey significant symbolic meaning through the forms they employ.

11.2.2 Language Styles – Edelman

The various styles of language usage convey meaning.[5] Such ceremonial activities of governments as election campaigns, committee hearings, diplomatic summits, or the public statements of high officials on policy decisions are all examples of public language designed implicitly to draw attention to matters of what should be unquestioned belief. It is the ritual aspects that call out or elicit these shared beliefs and values, not the substantive issues that may or may not be addressed at the time. In this sense even the use of radical rhetoric, with its threats, categorical statements, and idiomatic phrasing, while in appearance skeptical and critical of governments or the professed intentions of other segments of society, also serve the ritual function of inducing support for its own more radical values.

We can easily forget that these forms constitute presentational styles, which by their constant presence in political activity demonstrate how institutions and their spokespersons subtly reproduce characteristic beliefs and legitimacy about themselves and their roles. When experts on the economy or the law testify before government committees, that testimony is conveyed through the use of a formal language. These formal languages (many of them originating in the social sciences) tend to emphasize processes, problem-solving, and effective actions. Formal languages have the appearance of detachment. When statisticians express the relations of people to their society, they use formal objectifications which do not personalize their accounts. Such objectifications may make decision-making easier, unencumbered by exceptions and personal examples; and they may also serve to conceal the real issues at stake. In general, whenever there are problematic decisions to be made by professionals, public officials, or average citizens, they all tend to employ the conventions of formal language to present conflicting evidence and to generate alternative scenarios.

In addition to language conventions the physical setting, often in a special hearings room with formalities of furnishings and rules of order, acts as a presentational form that is meant to evoke public confidence in the fairness and legitimacy of the proceedings. All of which may, of course, simply serve to mask the real way in which decisions have been arrived at, behind closed doors. In any case, analysts of the symbolic modes of political practice such as Edelman believe that the consistent use of presentational styles indicates just how significantly public institutions depend upon the influence of language and physical setting. In this way institutions perform a dual role, simultaneously going about their assigned functions in society while shaping public meaning about the value of these functions.

11.2.3 Dominant Ideas – Barthes

Of the ideas that commonly make up our system of values and beliefs, some are at any given time dominant, more significant for us, than others. The French scholar Roland Barthes has provided a model for this process.[6] Art, we commonly believe, evolves through the activity of individual artists; but Barthes argues it is also regulated through the systematic actions of critics, galleries, curators, historians, dealers, and collectors. Through a variety of means these *control groups* exert a regulating force on the activity of artistic expression. Their power derives from their capacity to place upon works of art both meaning and value, including market value, which acts in turn as a frame of reference for both the public and the artists themselves.

Barthes proposed the model of control groups to show that the hierarchical arrangement of ideas attached to particular modes of cultural activity are neither arbitrary nor accidental. At what he called the *real level,* we find activities that from time to time combine to form a new set of ideas – all the personal and emotive circumstances involved in the production of a film, a painting, a book, or a play. Simultaneously, at a second level there are the *prevailing ideas* by which a product is conventionally understood and judged – prevailing notions about style, craft, or genre. And finally at a third level there are the indications of the significance gained as a result of *commentary* and *criticism,* matters which help to establish the product's connection to other works of comparable merit past and present.

Barthes' model describes the reflexive relation of artistic expression to the prevailing and dominant ideas of art as they are revealed by historians, collectors, and middlemen. Normally, a new system of ideas can be absorbed into an older system, while the old system continues to be modified by the process. Revolutions, in art at least, occur only when a new system of ideas emerges with sufficient strength to transcend the older system of ideas and judgments, often it seems when that older system allows too few options or imposes too many limits on artistic expression itself. Barthes believed his model to be capable of describing other activities as well; in his many books of social analysis he demonstrated how new myths relate to old myths, new fashions to older fashions, even new belief systems to older ones. In each case Barthes claimed that there is a reciprocal relationship between the influence of dominant ideas (we might say significant symbols) on cultural activity and the modifying influence of new cultural practices on the dominant ideas and attitudes themselves. This reflexive process is another example of the regulative or stabilizing role of symbolization, but one also highly sensitive to creativity and development as part of that process.

11.2.4 Symbol Regulation

Although Barthes' model comes close to showing us the constancy of the human factor in the diffusion and internalization of significant symbols, we tend to forget or underestimate the straightforward mechanisms for regulation in the control of reproduction. Patents, copyrights, and licensing all offer protection for the design and manufacture of material products (some of which can be symbols); but trademarks have the unique distinction of protecting a name, label, or symbol alone. There are even a few cautious ironies in this. Advertisers, for instance, succeed when they stimulate broad recognition and usage of brand names (if not the products themselves). However, when a brand name succeeds too well in becoming a household word, the result is often the loss of rights to the name itself. The Otis Elevator Company lost the trademark rights to the name "escalator" when the word came to be commonly used to refer to moving staircases other than its own. Likewise, aspirin, cellophane, linoleum, shredded wheat, and zipper all began as legal trademarks and ended up as generic words for other people's products. The effort to control through control of symbols is of course nothing new. But, if it is an indication of the perceived regulative power of symbols, the Xerox Corporation spends a lot of time and effort letting people know that they sell copying machines, not xeroxes; and the Coca-Cola Company retains an entire legal department for suing bars and restaurants who use the name "coke" for anything other than "the real thing."[7]

One can see evidence today of companies which are losing the battle to restrain usage in trademarks such as Kleenex, Band-Aid, and Scrabble, terms that have become nearly synonymous with our tissues, adhesive bandages, and crossword games. Then again, perhaps this is nothing more than a dollars and cents example of the defining and restraining role of symbols and symbolization.

11.3 Ritual Acts – A Final Remark

These observations on symbols and symbolization ought to be a reminder not only about the ritual character of our social symbolic world, but also about the ways in which we commonly observe it. "Whatever we have to say about social relationships," the anthropologist Edmund Leach has said, "is, in the last analysis, an interpretation of these 'ritual' acts."[8] The ritual nature of our symbolic interactions, including the role of our social institutions, should alert us again to how symbols shape and maintain reality. All commentators on others need to respect the limitations of observation and interpretation. What we think is an analysis of social reality may be, in fact, an analysis of its rituals, diffused through significant symbols, conventions of address, public ceremonies, special languages, dominant symbols, values, beliefs, and trademarks.

CHAPTER 12

Symbol Internalization

12.1 Internalization

12.1.1 Introduction

The final chapter in this section returns to the question of symbol internalization, the formative process that begins in childhood and is continually refashioned throughout life by the symbolic-linguistic system we call our culture. In addition to the broader roles of language, symbols, and social institutions, it is important to remember that the interplay of social and personal reality is also carried on through other modes such as interpersonal ties with family members, group activities, and through a range of informal relations. These informal interpersonal relations, more than any others, provide the earliest context through which we acquire our repertory of communicational skills for dealing with others and responding to them. Again, this is the way in which our private subjective experiences are, through symbolic interaction, transformed into communicable or intersubjective ones.

It is a commonplace idea in much modern philosophy that descriptions of the world are never completely separated from our activities in the world. They are reflexively related. Children, for instance, progressively come to understand "causality" through acknowledging that their bodily actions and surrounding objects are inseparably a part of each other. Their movements and the movements of those around them cause things to happen. What the child perceived first as a set of external relationships to her physical environment is transformed and internalized as mental conceptions with which she can now consider her relationship to things without the necessity of action.

In much the same way our knowledge of social institutions, codes, conventions, and other conceptual frameworks of our culture come to us first as external accompaniments to our actions and the actions of others, we gradually internalize. This process of *internalization* of our social world needs special emphasis, in part because it is the key to our development, socialization, and enculturation into a world of symbols, and in part because we as yet know so little about it.

12.1.2 Inner Speech – Vygotsky

The Soviet psychologist L.S. Vygotsky observed in very young children that overt speech frequently accompanies their actions.[1] Such talk, loud enough to be heard but directed only to themselves, forms a kind of running commentary on a child's own physical efforts. These early speech forms appear to serve mainly a signal function. It is at later stages of development that children discover the symbolic function of words and begin to utilize speech in the service of thinking. Speech and thought, Vygotsky proposed, serve different functions. First, as an external function, children use spoken language to communicate and to think. Then, these speech structures, which have been mastered through contact with the social environment, are internalized and continue to develop into the basic structures of thinking.

Vygotsky's work is critical of early behavioral psychologists who believed that thought was simply subaudible speech, a sort of silent talk. Thinking, Vygotsky argued, results from the successful internalizing of the uses of language which children experience as part of their social contact with others. The internalizing process, thus, comes to be different from speech and to serve a different function.

Vygotsky proposed that inner and external speech perform

radically different functions. *Inner speech* serves the ego in thinking; outer speech serves in social relations. The development of inner speech is a sort of secondary function acquired as a result of the child's contact with society. Like his mentor Pavlov, Vygotsky believed that inner speech formed the basis for a *second signal system,* separate from the *primary signal system* which Pavlov had identified in animal behavior. Vygotsky insisted on the importance of the social environment in the development of this second signal system of cognition. Again he stressed the reflexive manner in which the capacity for thought arises from our social relations.

12.1.3 Speechlessness – Furth

Furth provided some independent confirmation of the importance of the social context to thinking through his investigations of deaf children.[2] The deaf are linguistically deprived, yet their intelligence and maturity seem to be not basically different from that of the hearing. Younger deaf children perform less well on tests which require discovery procedures, but as they mature this deficiency lessens. Furth speculated that the deficit in young deaf children may be *motivational* and the result of their *social environment.* Verbal language provides the hearing child with a continuous source of information and attention. By contrast, the social world of deaf children must be contributed to by pointing, gestures, and pictures – things which parents of the deaf are not normally encouraged to do. Consequently, Furth says, "a deaf child is often seriously deficient in the knowledge of things familiar to hearing peers."[3] Deficiencies of the deaf, so often associated with the lack of a language, may well be due to deficiencies of *social experience,* particularly those that would provide the motivation for exploration, discovery, and independence. In fact, when provided with a rich social world, deaf children quickly develop the conceptual and symbolic capabilities we too often ascribe to linguistic competency alone. It is true that speech and thought are intertwined; but it is our social order and its stress on the verbal over the nonverbal which creates the illusion that there is no thinking without language. Both examples, then, speech acquisition as well as speechlessness, point to the importance of the total symbolic environment – rituals, symbols, language, and gestures – in our development and enculturation.

12.2 Especially Gestures – Tinbergen and Tinbergen

Observations on the parallel worlds of zoosemiotics (animal communication) and anthroposemiotics (human communication) have also pointed up the role that nonverbal modes, especially gestures, play in stabilizing – or destabilizing – the social process. The Nobel Prize winning ethologist, Nikolas Tinbergen, found in the mating behavior of gulls that many movements with a communicating or signalling function were the result of *motivation conflict* in the signaller.[4] Slight variations in the behavior of an intimidating partner (the male gull) could radically influence the behavior of a timid partner (the female gull). Thus, in the mating ritual the male must curb his own normally aggressive movements in order that the female can overcome her timidity in approaching the male. At early stages *ritual behaviors* help to stabilize this bonding process. By "facing away," potential partners avoid engaging in the straight look which could increase the anxiety of the timid partner. When unchecked by ritual behavior, the bonding process can produce what Tinbergen calls a motivational crisis, psychologically speaking, an *approach-avoidance syndrome*.

Ethologists have found it easy to utilize theories of ritual in their descriptions of animal behavior, in part because animals seldom interact as equals, and in part because of the close association they often find between nonverbal communication in animals and ritual forms of human behavior. Thus when Tinbergen applied his observations of social encounters in gulls to his wife's study of autistic children, the results suggested just how strongly the ritual gestures of the social environment may figure in the creation of motivational conflicts in humans.

Autistic children are typified by excessive timidity, by refusing most communication with others – avoidance of eye contact, direct body contact and so on, often resulting in a pattern of arrested speech, permanent social withdrawal and anxiety. *Psychogenic autism* – autism that is thought to be environmentally induced – the Tinbergens found to be the result of motivational conflicts in the child produced through his encounters with adults.[5] They found additionally that the behavior of autistic children was not notably different from other children. Normally timid children, for instance, display occasionally all the symptoms of permanently autistic children; and autistic children for their part naturally seek contact with adults and peers much as do normal children. An autistic child, they observed, will back onto the lap of a stranger whom it would not otherwise approach. So striking was the similarity of the bonding behavior of gulls and the socializing behavior of children that the Tinbergens were able to demonstrate how easily our *ways of presenting* ourselves to children, when they are too intrusive or too direct can produce motivational conflict leading to withdrawal, anxiety, even severe pathology.

In psychoanalysis, therapists often utilize the ritual of turning ones back to the analyst in an effort to diffuse the anxieties associated with the nonverbal dimension of *therapeutic encounters.* Tinbergen and others have noted that this procedure, where analysts remain seated behind and to the side of the client, seems to reduce some anxiety, but it also cuts off a range of observations useful to the therapist. By contrast, more recent therapies and some forms of psychoanalysis today acknowledge the fuller significance of nonverbal displays by allowing more direct visual and tactile interaction between clients and therapists. But, here too, therapists must be careful to find unthreatening ways of presenting themselves to their clients, a sort of therapeutic bonding ritual.

Through all these types of socializing ritual, the motivation to explore, discover, bond, and socially develop becomes successfully internalized in children. Or as in the case of psychogenic autism, the difficulty adults experience in understanding how their own socializing rituals appear threatening to excessively timid children can retard this process. Even the so-called "early retardation" of deaf children seems to be the result of their early formative experience with socializing rituals. A verbally biased society stressing oral-aural channels of information ought not to expect the same degree of motivation from children for whom the nonverbal mode may be the only mode they have – or as with autistics the most threatening one.

12.3 The Delta Factor – Percy

In all the cases that have been touched upon in this chapter – the experience of children mastering the transformation of inner speech into thought, the way that speechlessness deters but finally need not prevent the deaf from attaining cognitive capacities similar to the rest of us, even the struggle of autistic children to overcome a threatening world of words and gestures – there is a remarkable demonstration of how the many social rituals of symbol internalization contribute to the development of inter-subjective experience.

The American novelist, philosopher, and physician Walker Percy has analyzed a classic example of the transformation represented by symbol internalization, the celebrated case of Helen Keller, a deaf and blind child in Alabama at the end of the last century, who was able to overcome a sightless and soundless existence to acquire the capacity to read and write (braille) and even to master a halting form of speech, which she herself could not hear.[6] At the age of eight Helen Keller had a moment of discovery which telescoped the emergence of thought into a single pristine event. In her autobiography she wrote of this experience:

> We walked down the path to the well house, attracted by the fragrance of the honeysuckle with which it was covered. Someone was drawing water and my teacher placed my hand under the spout. As the cool stream gushed over one hand, she spelled into the other the word *water,* first slowly then rapidly. I stood still, my whole attention fixed upon the motion of her fingers. Suddenly I felt a misty consciousness as of something forgotten – a thrill of returning thought; and somehow the mystery of language was revealed to me. I knew then that "w-a-t-e-r" meant the wonderful cool something that was flowing over my hand. That living word awakened my soul, gave it light, hope, joy, set it free! There were barriers still, it is true, but barriers that could in time be swept away.[7]

What happened to Helen Keller was something like a discovery of the *negative liberating power of symbols.* The event at the well marked her passage from a world of signals – where the words tapped onto her hand meant the thing named, food to eat, water to drink, and so on – to a simultaneous world of symbols – where the name of the thing and the thing itself were related yet independent of each other and where the name became applicable to other phenomena both real and imaginary. Percy explained this passage from a signal-dominated environment to a symbol-liberating one by what he calls *the delta factor.* Specifically human behavior results from the capacity language provides us to negate and transcend the immediate environment: for Helen Keller at the well house the water was no longer just the water "out there"; the word "water" was no longer just the touch spelled out on her hand; and she was no longer simply an organism responding only to the needs and gratifications of immediately given circumstances.

For Percy, the delta factor (from the Greek letter Δ, the triangle signifying irreducibility) describes that as-yet-unexplained process by which we come to recognize the nonlinear, multidirectional status of the linguistic symbol. Recognition of the power of the symbol, which comes upon most of us gradually as we develop and which came upon Helen Keller with such suddenness, constitutes an awareness that the naming of things and relations is a form of knowledge and power over the environment itself. It is this linguistic-symbolic development, Walker Percy believes, that provides the basis for our *intersubjectivity* – for our capacity to act in ways not immediately subject to the demands of our environment and our capacity to grasp simultaneously the meaning of an experience for others as well as for ourselves.

Helen Keller was deaf and blind and, in the beginning at least, speechless. She might well have remained so. Instead, she was able to break through into what she describes as a world of language. The role of her teacher in this transformation ought to make us more aware of how many of our efforts at instructing, healing, and relating are aimed at the development and repair of our intersubjectivity. With much assistance almost all of us do break through into the world of language. Yet, our symbolic-linguistic world continues to resist our efforts to explain it and never ceases to command our efforts to grasp it more fully.

12.4 A Final Note

In these first twelve chapters we have moved more deeply into the relation of social reality and personal reality, not only to describe it in greater detail, but to offer some fundamental explanations as well. Many of these explanations have attempted to identify the role or function of communication – how it is used, for what, and why it is necessary. So strongly has this search for roles and functions influenced past studies of communication that these *explanations by function* are never really absent today from our understanding of the communication process. At the same time this emphasis on roles and functions is not so much a quest for a single way of explaining communication as it is a quest for a consistent way of explaining some of it.

The processes of diffusion, feedback, symbolization, and reflexion that the preceding chapters have portrayed as central features of communication form the background for the rest of the text. The chapters that follow attempt to show how these basic concepts can be useful for analyzing and understanding our shared experiences as members of a culture and, even more optimistically, the culturally defined and constrained experience of others.

PART FOUR

Bias — The Semiotic Web

"The whole point of a semiotic approach to culture," anthropologist Clifford Geertz says, is "to aid us in gaining access to the conceptual world in which our subjects live so that we can, in some extended sense of the term, converse with them."[1] It is a large generalization, but much of the material that follows in these latter chapters shares with a semiotic approach to culture and communication the goal of (1) gaining access to the conceptual world of others and of (2) facilitating conversation with them and with ourselves.

Unlike the fish which is said to be unaware of the water in which it swims, we often come to know something of the encompassing quality of our own cultural environment by contrast and comparison with other cultures. By contrasting and comparing we recognize that there are different sets of meanings accompanying the preoccupations and activities of diverse human groupings and, within these groupings, we can discern other sorts of differences as we compare one place to another or take account of the passage from one time period to another. Cultures consist of these groupings and the differences brought about through the evolution of shared concepts and beliefs (ones that people commonly recognize as meaningful) and of shared patterns of interaction (ones that people commonly perform).

The task of gaining access to the conceptual world of others then involves understanding how these systems of shared meanings and concepts relate to the various preoccupations, activities, and practices that occur in a culture. Swiss linguist Ferdinand de Saussure compared this task to that of studying the reflexive relationship between language and speech.[2] Shifts in language occur or evolve through the day-to-day activity of speech; and speech in turn depends for its power of communication on the commonly shared rules and coded meanings of language, which, while they too evolve, do so in a systematic and largely imperceptible manner. For any given language it is possible to identify these relations between the actual concrete speech situations and the higher order of codes and concepts which provides the rules of combination. Saussure believed that there are equivalent relations between actual practices and activities in which people engage and the higher order of codes, roles, and concepts which steer and orient these practices. Because we can identify codes and practices at work in a culture, it is possible to distinguish similarities and differences from culture to culture in much the same way that it is possible to compare and contrast different languages. The study of these similarities and differences (and their modification) is what is known as a semiotic approach to culture and to the role of communication therein. This provides the starting point for the chapters to follow.

CHAPTER 13

Perceptual Bias

13.1 Systems of Latent Meaning

13.1.1 Introduction

When we perceive we do so with anticipation and with prejudice. Anticipation and prejudice refer to the role of preconceptions in all our activities and to the continual process of perceptual modification through feedback. To make this clearer we can take the conventional distinction that is made about awareness levels in perception. At the first level of awareness the dominant relationship we find is with concrete physical objects, processed especially through our sense of sight. At this first level, reality seems to be imposed upon our senses. It is necessary to re-emphasize that reality "seems" to impose itself upon our senses because, even at this level, when more than one physical object is encountered in the visual field, our first level perceptions respond by modifying the relationship of these objects to one another. If for instance one object oscillates around another one that does not move, we may perceive both objects as moving toward and away from each other. Such curiosities of perception seem to indicate that, even at the first level, we perceive *in context.* Whenever there is more than one item to handle, our perceptual apparatus attempts to describe them in relationship to one another.[1]

By contrast, second level awareness involves the assigning of meaning and value to experience. At this level perceptions seem to be imposed upon reality. This is most obvious in the way different cultures emphasize different attitudes toward behavior and belief; consequently, the same pressures that produce similar attitudes or conformities within a culture are also responsible for the differences from one culture to another. Second level awareness is maintained by its feedback link to actual experience, and thus is itself continuously modified by this feedback. The result is what social scientists call a systematic differentiation of perspective, whereby every culture comes to have what might be called its own culturally based ways of seeing, or bias. Bias in this usage does not refer to psychological matters (such as personal or group prejudice, stereotyping, and the like), but to the way in which our second-level awareness constitutes a shared set of coded meanings and values by which cultures implicitly stabilize and orient the interactions of its members and in terms of which its members find shared meaning in them. Bias consists of the multiplicity of codes – unconscious as well as conscious, latent and manifest – found in a culture at any given time. Obviously, pluralistic cultures such as our own Western cultures may seem to have many more such codes in operation at a given time, and to have codes in greater conflict with one another, than less pluralistic cultures. But even in pluralistic cultures such systems of codes may define and constrain our thinking and our actions far more than is commonly acknowledged.

13.1.2 The Appointment in Samarra

Novelist W. Somerset Maugham tells an archetypal tale about an encounter between Death and one of its appointed victims which illustrates the previous point.[2] In Baghdad a servant who had been sent to market to buy provisions returned home empty-handed and anxiously explained to his master that, while in the marketplace, he had been jostled by a woman in the crowd; and when he had turned to look at her he saw that it was no woman but Death itself who had jostled him. Death, the servant said, had returned his stare and made a threatening gesture. Now, the servant pleaded, he must flee. So the master lent the servant a horse and the servant set out at great speed for Samarra, to be as far as possible from Death by nightfall. Then the master himself went to the market-place and when he too saw Death there he approached and asked why Death had made a threatening gesture to his servant that morning. But it was not a threatening gesture, Death protested. It was a gesture of surprise. I was astonished to see your servant in Baghdad this morning when I have an appointment with him tonight in Samarra.

13.1.3 Gestures – Birdwhistell

Gestures form an important system of coded meaning. Gestural systems normally appear concurrent with the flow of speech, but they can also appear independently of what is said. By filming and reproducing the second-by-second body movements of ordinary interaction, the kinesics researcher Ray Birdwhistell was able to show that a series of movements normally thought to contain little meaning of consequence was in fact regular, orderly, and predictable parts of behavior.[3] His analysis revealed that such gestures as nods and sweeps of the head, blinks, movements of the chin, lips, shoulders, arms, hands, and even fingers could be isolated and organized into components and combinations much like that of ordinary language. Much as the phone and morpheme combine to produce words, Birdwhistell proposed that kine and kinemorph provided the formal parts of gestural language. Gestural language may exist independently of speech as a separate pattern (macrokinesics) and it can also accompany speech as a sort of para-language (parakinesics) which supplies additional clues about the context of the speech activity.

Research of this sort, which focuses such minute attention on our nonverbal and largely unconscious behavior, is making it increasingly difficult for us to go on regarding the process of communication in quite the same commonsense ways we have been used to. Seeing, as Erving Goffman proposed, is not believing; it is at best reconfirming. Intriguingly, both Goffman and Birdwhistell in their work with patients in mental institutions have suggested that much that disturbs the mentally ill – what may in fact contribute to driving them insane – comes from the perceived conflict between what we say and what our gestures betray about us.[4] Like Somerset Maugham's parable, the science of subconscious gestures points to the presence of a larger system of meanings with which we interact. Gestures are an important component in what we see. They are, in a sense, an indication of our bias.

13.1.4 Proxemics – Hall

Parallel with the microempirical world uncovered by Birdwhistell, Edward Hall has described how we communicate meaning through organizing space and manipulating distance.[5] We all recognize these conventions when our expectations about them are violated. We expect conversations, for instance, to occur at arm's length. When we see people talking at closer range we may suspect either conspiracy or intimacy. Hall found that North Americans attribute social meaning to four types of perceived distance, which he labelled public distance (more than 13 feet), social distance (four to twelve feet), personal distance (two to four feet), and intimate distance (six to eighteen inches). Each of these is further divided into close and far. At *close personal distance* people are able to physically touch each other, while *far personal distance* describes that distance where two people are outside easy physical contact. *Close social distance* seems to be the distance at which most normal business relations in our culture occur. The further the social distance the more likely the formality of the occasion or the greater the difference in perceived social status between the people involved.

Actors and confidence men, of course, have always been aware of these boundaries and their possibilities for manipulation. The anxiety or confusion we experience when we feel the appropriate distance for an occasion has been violated makes us vulnerable to manipulation. It also underscores the way in which distance does indeed provide us with a continuous source of nonverbal meaning.

Hall believes such conventions can be a major source of misunderstanding in the modern world where cultural boundaries are crossed so frequently and with little preparation. The businessman, for instance, who arrives on time in North America may be showing respect, but the same behavior in South America may be seen as a sign of haste and even, therefore, a sign of disrespect toward the other. Time, like distance, contains its own differently coded meanings and values.[6]

Despite their role in misunderstanding, Birdwhistell and Hall both emphasize that kinesic and proxemic codes serve primarily to stabilize meaning, providing us with continuous subconscious reassurance that our perceptions about the world still hold. Such forms of metacommunication occasionally may mislead us; but more often their role is simply to reinforce.

13.2 Systems of Manifest Meaning

13.2.1 The Visual Image – Gombrich

At more manifest but still nonverbal levels of communication we frequently encounter a variation on perceptual bias known as the *perceptual temptation.* Perceptual temptation refers to our tendency to believe that what we feel as a result of the expression of others is somehow what they felt in giving rise to that expression in the first place. E.H. Gombrich pointed to examples such as the accompanying cartoon as graphic illustrations of how easily and confidently the perceptual temptation is entertained by both the senders and the receivers of nonverbal communication.[7]

Gombrich noted that experiments conducted in Germany by Reinhard Kraus seem to confirm the view expressed by the cartoon. When experimental subjects were asked to convey ideas or emotions through drawing abstract forms, the guesses on the part of others were found to be random. Only when those doing the guessing were given a list of possible meanings did their performance improve. The shorter the list of alternatives, the more accurately they managed to guess.

Nonverbal forms of art seem to be especially vulnerable to this state of affairs. When we speak of art as communication, we sometimes imply that the emotions the artist experienced in creating the work are similar if not identical to those that the viewer of the

Drawing by CEM; © 1961 The New Yorker Magazine, Inc.

work receives. Such simplistic notions or models of the communication process fail totally to account for what Gombrich calls the *beholder's share,* "the contribution we make to any representations from the stock of images stored in our mind."[8] What a visual representation means to the viewer is governed by his past experience and current knowledge and by what Gombrich calls the influence of the code, the caption, and the context. Again, this points to how actual experience may be defined and constrained by the meaning codes make available to us.

Closely allied to the perceptual temptation is the *representational temptation* – the tendency to believe that the visual image appears as it does because that is how the eye sees it. The famous woodcut done by the German artist Albrecht Dürer is a powerful reminder of just how strongly vision is prejudiced by preconceptions. When Dürer made his woodcut of a rhinoceros in 1515, he relied on evidence received secondhand from travellers and supplemented by what he already knew of the mythic dragon with armored body. The result was a stunning image which profoundly influenced the art world. And as we can see from the engraving

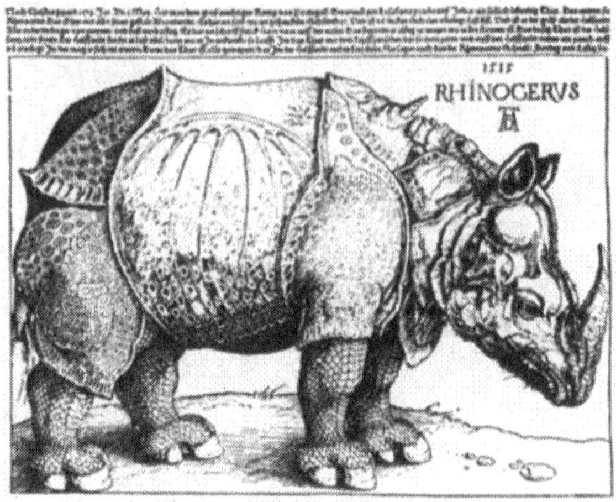

Dürer: *Rhinoceros. 1515, woodcut*

Heath: *Rhinoceros of Africa. 1789, engraving*

African rhinoceros

(Adapted from E. H. Gombrich, *Art and Illusion*, Princeton University Press; Dürer rhinoceros reprinted by permission of New York Public Library; Heath's rhinoceros reprinted by permission of Princeton University Press; photo reprinted by permission of Conzett and Huber) done from real life in 1789, two centuries later, it was still possible to find strong hints and stylistic traces of Dürer's original.

As a representation of reality the visual image is part of a symbolic system of coded meaning. Gombrich's brilliant example of Dürer's influence on graphic artists shows how, when we see, we are guided in part by what we have experienced and by our preconceptions and accepted conventions about how things should appear.[9] Dürer may never have seen a live rhinoceros; but the influence of his one image defined and constrained the artist's vision almost until the age of the photograph.

13.2.2 The Verbal Image – Whorf

During the time the anthropologist Benjamin Lee Whorf worked for a fire insurance company, he noticed that factory workers tended to be careful around gasoline drums they knew to be full, but around empty gasoline drums they smoked openly and discarded cigarette butts without concern.[10] Empty gasoline drums are, if anything, more dangerous because they contain potentially explosive vapors. But as the workers saw it, containers that were known to be empty conveyed less of a sense of danger than full ones. Deceptive preconceptions of this sort can also be a guide to behavior. In this case the caption "gasoline drums" combined with the analogy of "empty" suggested to Whorf's factory workers the lack rather than the presence of a hazard. And, as Whorf's fire insurance company realized, altering these sorts of attitudes and the behavior they encourage can be agonizingly difficult.

13.2.3 Image and Opinion – Berger

"Every image," John Berger says, "embodies a way of seeing."[11] When renaissance art developed the convention of perspective – the idea that the viewer's eye was the point into which all appearances converged – it created the popular belief that the viewer was the center of the world. Only the appearance of the camera disturbed the power of that illusion. The camera, by capturing the same scene from many different point of view, demonstrated that there was no center and, thus, no one privileged point of view.

Unfortunately, Berger feels, the images that camera reproduction made possible have been used predominately in modern society to restrict rather than open up points of view. Berger points to publicity as an example of the effort to guide opinion through restricting point of view. Publicity, unlike art, is always presented in a sort of visual future tense. It is only the illusion of choice that forms of publicity such as advertising offer us, says Berger. The capacity of the camera to provide us with many perspectives and, therefore, potentially to offer us many choices serves in advertising publicity to provide images through which we are presented with systematic standards of what is desirable and what is not desirable. A code is what is really being marketed. In a pessimistic way we could say that such modern uses of coded images are meant to narrow rather than broaden choice. All of which leads Berger to caution us about the essential falseness of opinion or judgment that is based upon the manipulation of images.

13.3 Conclusion

Coded meanings and concepts that make up any given culture at a given time provide it with a repertory of values. The uses of gesture, distance, verbal and nonverbal images all construct the semiotic web in which we exist. It may be difficult to accept the idea that the shared meaning of our communication is already given by the codes of the culture we inhabit and is changed only imperceptibly by our actions. Perhaps it would be enough to say that, when we communicate, it is this semiotic web that provides the range of interpretations and meanings that we habitually find therein.

CHAPTER 14

Interactional Bias

14.1 A Grammar of Situations

14.1.1 Introduction

Our sensitivity to the situations we experience depends in part upon culturally coded meanings and values which, because they comprise commonly shared expectations, seldom come to our attention in everyday encounters. In fact, so unconscious are we of such conventions that some researchers believe they cannot be found in our specific experiences at all but only through careful observations of *the way in which we experience.* In other words our ways of experiencing are of greater significance than the content of our experience; and some go so far as to claim that these ways of experiencing are inseparable from our habitual patterns of social interaction and our habitual use of communication modes. As noted earlier, primary modes of interaction normally refer to direct or face-to-face relationships, whereas secondary modes depend upon some sort of technological means (printing, telephonics, telemedia, and so on). Although controversial, it can be argued that these secondary modes also provide subtle forms of constraint on our thoughts and actions. Furthermore, because new technological means of communication offer new potentials for thought and action, secondary modes can be a source of change in preferred ways of experience, or what might be called interactional biases.

14.1.2 A Note on Primary Modes – Frames and Meanings

In earlier chapters we touched upon primary modes of interaction and identified the preponderance of what one group of researchers called complementary and symmetrical patterns that orient and constrain our interpersonal behavior. Therapists have been especially aware of such habitual patterns (or biases) in our interaction and have produced some of the best evidence for the defining and constraining influence of such patterns on our thought and action. Therapists, for example, have frequently noted that a client's awareness of his or her troubled behavior patterns can sometimes be achieved only once the perception of that behavior has been changed. The client's perception is a form of framing and, since every frame involves a labelling and valuing of experience, therapists sometimes attempt to modify a client's habitual framing patterns through reframing them. Therapeutic reframing, Paul Watzlawick claims, is an effort "to change the conceptual and/or emotional setting or viewpoint in relation to which a situation is experienced and to place it in another frame which fits the 'facts' of the same concrete situation equally well or even better, and thereby changes its entire meaning."[1]

Watzlawick recounts the treatment of a man with a bad stammer who was faced with the opportunity of working as a salesman. This new opportunity had caused him renewed concern over his speech defect and this, in turn, brought him to seek therapeutic help. The therapist, finding no other personality problems and not wishing to dissuade the client from his newfound career, proceeded to try to reframe the situation for him. On the one hand, the therapist noted that salesmen are often disliked for their slick and insistent talk. In fact, they may even be distrusted for this reason. On the other hand, people are unusually patient and solicitous with handicapped people. Therefore, what the client might view as a handicap in other circumstances could have certain benefits in this particular situation. Thus, the therapist reframed a situation of potential anxiety for the client into one in which the source of the anxiety could have a positive role. What is changed as a result of the therapeutic reframing is not the situation itself, but the meaning and value habitually attributed to it.

The benefits we may gain from a new perspective seem to show how primary patterns of interaction do define and constrain our actions; and how the meaning attached to such patterns can also change through adaptations, both gradual and abrupt. In fact, the changes that the interactional therapies claim to make do not alter our patterns of interaction and experience so much as they help us to recognize and modify how we value them.

14.2 A Grammar of Orientations

14.2.1 Secondary Modes of Interaction – McLuhan

Communication technologies also enter into our patterns of interaction and experience. In fact, so great is this influence thought to be that such technologies are believed to form an entire secondary mode of human activity. As participants in a culture steeped in technology we sometimes have trouble acknowledging the influence of our own technological environment. Yet the elements of that environment surround us: mass production technologies place a wealth of goods and services within reach of the majority; transportation technologies connect us easily to distant places; and communication technologies provide an endless store of information and entertainment resources. In fact, so powerfully present does the technological environment appear that we can fairly raise questions about the *cumulative effects* of technology upon our characteristic patterns of thought and interaction.

Questions about the *patterns* of interaction are quite different from the lengthy scholarship concerned with assessing the *impact* of technological innovation. Technological impact, or effects, studies often lead to questions of whether technology is really a *determining factor* in social and cultural life. When Marshall McLuhan, for instance, declared that technologies such as the telephone and the computer transform our sense organs, he was accused of attributing too much impact or effect to the technologies themselves. He was, on occasion, called a technological determinist. Yet, with a little hindsight, what McLuhan seems to have been drawing our attention to is the extent to which the introduction of some new means of communication alters the way we habitually interact with the social environment. McLuhan seems to have been intrigued with the subtler changes in sensibilities that arose in concert with new communication technologies rather than with measurement of their brute effects.[2]

14.2.2 Technology and Culture – Innis

The Canadian economist Harold Innis observed that changes in the patterns of interaction which accompany communication technologies are generally so widely distributed in a society or culture and result so deliberately from the use of that technology that we often fail to see the way the technology *orients* these interactions.[3] Innis himself mapped out some of the interaction patterns brought about by the predominant channels through which a society's information is moved and managed. The changed orientations brought about by this circuitry could be analyzed by asking certain kinds of questions. Did the information in a culture, society, or region move from periphery to center, from the center out, or in a complete circuit? Did a society value information as a scarce resource by storing it up or did they treat it as an abundant commodity? Did information move into increasingly larger spheres, pressing the borders of a culture outward or, conversely, drawing it inward?

Innis found that two general orientations were present in a culture at any time: an orientation stressing *short-distance patterns* of communication, which depend largely on direct interpersonal contacts and emphasize local influence and local decision-making; and an orientation stressing *long-distance patterns* of communication, which rely upon communication technologies and emphasize constituencies of people related by national, professional, or other special interests not confined to the local level. When long-distance orientations predominate, Innis believed, it led not only to the deterioration of many localized features of cultural and social life, but replacing local sources of information with distant ones alters how and what people think about as well. A predominance of short-distance communication, by contrast, could promote insularity, parochialism, and the systematic withdrawal from contact with others that prefigures and sets the atmosphere for periods of prejudice and superstition.[4]

Innis referred to these interactional orientations as biases. Too much of one or not enough of the other produce pathological symptoms within a culture. He noted too how such biases could affect relationships between cultures of unequal size and strength. When communication media from the United States press the borders of its own culture outward, the occasion could become a threatening one at the margins of Canadian or Mexican society. Similarly, when a country such as Canada plans to extend modern media services (such as television through satellites) to its own remote north, the indigenous Indian and Inuit peoples living there must consider carefully the consequences of this new orientation toward a culture of disproportionately greater size and strength.

14.2.3 Technology and Community – Carey

James Carey, a student of Innis' work, has proposed that when long-distance forms of transportation or communication are improved (increased speed and decreased cost over greater distance), this improvement results in the deterioration of other social and cultural features.[5] In this case, local and regional forms of community are threatened, even replaced, by quasi-national ones in the form of associations and professional and other special interest groupings. One consequence of this is that members of minority cultures can be weaned away from local loyalties by the introduction of new means of communication.

14.2.4 Technology and Thought – Goody

Jack Goody observed some intriguing consequences of the introduction of written forms of mathematics among the LoDagaa people of Northern Ghana.[6] Although the LoDagaa already possessed an oral system of counting (basically forms of addition and subtraction), the introduction of schooling in the 1950s brought with it the use of charts and tables for multiplication and division and the use of written notation for figuring complex sums. Goody was able to observe the ancient and modern systems side by side because many of the non-schooled LoDagaa continued to use the oral system, while the schooled LoDagaa preferred pencil and paper. Goody noted that, when he asked them to count for him, the non-schooled LoDagaa always insisted on counting something concrete – money, cows, children, while the schooled LoDagaa were more willing to count in the abstract. The oral system was quicker and somewhat more accurate for adding and subtracting; but the familiarity of the schooled LoDagaa with memorized multiplication tables and written forms of division gave them a significant advantage.

The introduction of multiplication and division through tables to be memorized or, as is more common today, incorporated into mechanical and electronic calculators, generates a new system of communicative acts. New technological means of communication, or computation, are an important source for new types of communicative acts. Goody has labelled such technologies as *technologies of the intellect,* in order to emphasize the way in which they provide new orientations for human thinking and new potentials for human interaction. We should not, however, forget that new means of communication (or computation) create limitations as well as potentials by their restricted availability and through their restricted control by special groups.

14.2.5 A Final Note on Technology

These points of view on how communication technology shapes interaction patterns and experience are part of a movement away from viewing communication channels simply and strictly as a means to know or to be entertained. Our senses also serve as a means to interact with our environment and our means of communication and the infrastructure they create by their emphasis on local or longer-distance orientations do influence and even significantly alter our patterns of interaction. Likewise, technologies that provide for the movement and storage of information (writing, notation and classification procedures, computing, etc.)

do so in ways that both change and habitualize our thinking and our interactions. Some greater awareness of these consequences of technological development may, in fact, lie behind the recent interest in *appropriate technologies* and the demand that we try to make political decisions about technology in light of the sorts of interaction they seem likely to enhance and inhibit.

14.3 The Concept of Interactional Bias

14.3.1 Bateson's Model of Calibration and Feedback

In all societies and cultures, Bateson has noted, people employ routines or methods to guide their habitual interaction with one another and with their environment; and these routines are continually adjusted as a result of actual experiences.[7] Calibration (or setting) and feedback are basic components of such routines. *Calibration* refers to the way in which we habitually classify or organize our patterns of interaction in specific ways. *Feedback* refers to the self-corrective information received as a result of repeated experience. It represents Wiener's principle of conservation at work in our interactions. Calibration provides the "setting" we give to our expectations about that reality. It is the basis of our anticipations and prejudices. Calibration classifies feedback and feedback, in turn, may bring about a change in calibration. Without a system of such calibrations we could not hope to make sense of the variety and volume of experiential information that reaches our senses in the form of feedback.

Consider, for example, the classic case of temperature control in a heated house with occupants. Temperature is continuously monitored through a mechanical thermostat which controls the fuel supply to the furnace. The thermostat receives feedback from the environment of the house; and since the thermostat also contains a calibration or setting, when the temperature rises above that setting the thermostat turns the furnace off; when it falls below the setting, the furnace is turned back on. The setting of the thermostat in turn is controlled by the residents of the house; and this setting depends upon the feedback received by the sense organs of the residents themselves.

The setting on the thermostat and the temperature threshold of the human residents both constitute the *bias of the system*. Since humans have different thresholds – convalescing patients may have a lower threshold than healthy outdoors types – the residents of the house may have to mutually work this setting out as conditions demand. Thus, in Bateson's model of interaction both the technological interactions involving the thermostat and furnace and the intersubjective interactions involving the negotiated needs of the residents can be viewed as an interrelated process of alternation between calibration and feedback.

14.3.2 Conclusion

Bateson's model describes a situation not unlike the relation of codes and practices, where coded meanings or values continue to guide practices until such time as the feedback from the actual experiences bring about some altered value. The example above may seem a bit contrived because the residents are seemingly limited to adjusting the range of values on a thermostat. But it is useful in pointing up the way in which a technology by its presence provides new potentials and also places limits on interaction. When we perceive a need for more warmth, we do not simply light a fire; and we normally do not act without some deference to the needs of others.

Perhaps what is implied by the model is that we are not prisoners of our interactional biases. Therapy is an example of how we can modify our primary modes (cooperation is another); and the introduction of new technological means (such as the introduction of central heating in northern Europe after World War II, or literacy into a preliterate society, or new communication technologies almost everywhere in the past few decades) indicate that secondary modes of interaction can and do alter previous patterns of experience and habits of mind.

CHAPTER 15

Representational Bias

15.1 Introduction

All our representations of reality are closely tied to the system of coded meanings through which specific cultures and societies classify and reproduce their distinctive practices.[1] From within our own Western and specifically North American context, it is tempting to think that the representations we encounter, through the sketch or the photograph for instance, are straightforward records of what actually existed at the time and the place they were produced. But as the case of Dürer's rhinoceros demonstrates, we produce representations and we interpret them largely in terms of past experience and knowledge. If we add to this the considerable influence of narrative styles and framing devices on media presentation, as well as the types of communication acts made possible by the technologies themselves, it becomes evident that what is being reproduced through these means and modes is not a copy of reality, but copies of copies of copies . . . which at some point have their basis in the system of shared codes and meanings. This is a central point of semiotic scholarship – to make clear the ways in which our representations always depend upon some shared system of classification which codes provide. Classification, we could say, provides the bias of our representations.

15.2 Facts and Representation

15.2.1 Representativeness – Tversky

When the psychologists Tversky and Kahneman investigated how people assess the probability of uncertain events or the value of uncertain quantities they found that people tend to rely on a few common formulas or recipes to reduce such complex problems to simpler judgmental operations.[2] Such formulas, or "heuristics" as Tversky calls them, in general are useful devices; but since we use them intuitively they can also be thought of as systematic forms of bias in judgment. One such heuristic device is our tendency to make judgments by representativeness.

Typically, Tversky observed, intuitive judgments are dominated by a belief in *local representativeness* – by the proportions of the localized sample without regard for the size of the sample itself. Tversky asked subjects to judge whether a large hospital with many births or a small hospital with fewer births would be more likely to have days on which the rate of boy births exceeded the average (which is 50%). Most subjects thought the likelihood to be the same for either hospital despite the fundamental statistical fact that a larger sample is less likely than a small sample to stray from the 50% average. We commonly believe, it seems, that such averages occur equally in all samples regardless of their size.

Gamblers are perennial dupes of this same fallacy of classification. When, after observing a long run of red at the roulette wheel, the gambler believes black is now due, he commits the error of viewing chance as a self-correcting process in which the equilibrium of black and red is restored. Such a view stems from the belief that the global characteristics of chance (in roulette an equal occurrence of red and black) will be demonstrated in each local case (that is, at each roulette wheel). The significance of such intuitive beliefs is not lost, of course, on those who operate the gaming tables.

It should be noted that it is not only ordinary people and gamblers who rely on these intuitive schemes. Experts use them too. When researchers construct hypotheses out of the results of a questionaire or population sample without regard for the size of the sample they similarly fall victim to the "law of small numbers," the belief that small samples with significant results are equivalent to larger samples. Such a belief, which is most consequential in the case of public opinion polls, Tversky believes "leads to the selection of samples of inadequate size and to over-interpretation of findings."[3]

When representativeness creates the illusion of validity, it can be very difficult to correct. Many personnel managers continue to rely upon clinical interviews for various purposes in selecting and dealing with employees, even though the literature of the field shows that such interviews are highly unreliable. Similarly, Tversky and Kahneman observed that flight training instructors fell under the influence of local patterns of learning when they observed that students who were praised for good landings did poorly on the next try, while those who were harshly criticized after a poor landing performed better the next time. The trainers reached the conclusion that punishment is more effective than reward. Such a conclusion flies in the face of the phenomenon of regression toward the mean – the statistical likelihood that a good performance will be followed by bad performance rather than another good one, and vice versa. Failure to understand the effects of regression, Tversky and Kahneman observe somewhat sadly, too often leads us to overestimate the effects of punishment and to underestimate the effects of reward.

The educational implications of this last point are far-reaching. It has been observed, for instance, that the failure of young children to perform speech acts they could previously do without error probably indicates that the child is beginning to master the higher-order rules that govern speaking. Hence, if we punish rather than reward children on such occasions it may be that we encourage continued mimicry and discourage their efforts to master the rules for themselves.

Again, all these examples of how classification problems can lead to systematic error should alert us to the presence and influence of representational bias in all our habitual observations.

15.2.2 Objectivity and Neutrality

15.2.2.1 Experimenter Bias – Terrace

The problem of estimating the impact of evidence implicates the observer as well as the observations themselves. Herbert Terrace, who devoted years to teaching a chimpanzee to use sign language, described how our commitment to proving correct an idea or hypothesis can blind us to its falseness as systematically as more intuitive schemes.[4] After four years of working with a single chimpanzee, Terrace and a team of researchers became disenchanted with what they thought was positive evidence of the chimp's language-learning ability when they began to study the extensive videotapes they had kept of their own experiments. What they found was that fully 90% of the signing behavior on the part of the chimp came in response to similar sign gestures by the trainers. Half of these responses were imitations of signs used in the questions asked by the trainers and many more seemed to be imitations of signs the trainers had unconsciously started but not completed.

Even more disturbing, when Terrace examined a now famous science documentary on the chimp Washoe (*The First Signs of Washoe*) he found that the documentarist consistently had edited the episodes so that the initial prompting of the trainers were not seen. The uncut version of these same episodes revealed that all the more complicated displays of signing by the chimp were imitations of similar signs just made by the trainers themselves. These findings, of course, demonstrate difficulties with the classification of observations on the part of the experimenters. As an indication of the talents of chimpanzees, it might be possible to conclude that their nonverbal powers of observation were perhaps greater, if less focused on the specifics of sign language, than their trainers assumed. Documentaries that cover such experiments may be doing nothing worse than mimicking the various forms of science they report on; but as *The First Signs of Washoe* testifies, when documentarists show us only the results, they risk compounding the evidence they claim to be merely presenting. Such incidents seem to point up the need for greater self-consciousness about the communicational process on the part of both scientists and documentarists, something chimps seem already to have mastered.

15.2.2.2 Documentarist Bias – Birdwhistell

Kinesics researcher Ray Birdwhistell noticed that the cameramen he used to film the gestures and interactions of people in public places sometimes avoided certain scenes or displays without being able to explain why they had done so.[5] One otherwise professional cameraman, while filming the activity around a Parisian newsstand, abruptly ceased filming for no apparent reason. When the film was later analyzed, the last episode revealed what appeared to be a prostitute engaging in a "pick-up" of a client. Though the cameraman had not consciously made the connection, he had nonetheless edited a scene which contained, from his own later admission, items in conflict with his beliefs.

Experiments such as these and the candor with which some social scientists have dealt with them gradually bring us to grips with Susanne Langer's warning that "the way a question is asked limits and disposes the ways in which any answer – right or wrong – can be given."[6] If cameraman and social scientist can each reveal errors in the observation of each other, we must seriously wonder if other practitioners, such as news reporters, news cameramen, or editors may not be similarly implicated.

The classical objective inquirer, Thrasymachus, in his reporting of events, claimed to be a neutral and value-free observer of his world. The ideal of inquiry represented by the ancient Greek is a worthy one; but the complexities of judgment required in most types of inquiry seem to cast considerable doubt upon their practicality as strategies for dealing with problems of representation. If as the Glasgow Media Group assert, television uses less than fifty shots and variations to bring us the news, we must begin to wonder whether such standardization, in addition to stabilizing the representations we receive, does not also make us less conscious of alternative perspectives and, therefore, less conscious as producers and consumers of how news is always news from some point of view.[7] Similarly, studies of the structure of news reports in Scandinavian countries have indicated that the news report strongly resembles the linguistic structure of traditional fairy tales – all of which ought to alert us to the difficulties we face in our uses of current media to provide representations of our social reality.[8]

15.3 Facts and Contexts

15.3.1 Facts as symbols

If classification and observation compound the judgment of experts, we should be aware of the consequences for the general public. When for instance a scientist reports to a government committee that 90% of the scientists who ever lived are alive today, he or she may only intend to stress the continuing role of the scientific community in our lives. However, when a reporter, or a teacher, repeats this "fact" without also pointing out that this is a statistic that was as true fifty, one hundred, or even one hundred and fifty years ago as it is today he or she may unwittingly contribute to a public sense of disproportion about the presence of the scientific community in our own time. Whenever scientists or reporters convey the results of their analyses or observations to a larger audience the facts they report are transformed from mere representations of reality into representations which can also promote one side or another of that reality. Such representations, James Carey has noted, serve to promote in subtle ways aspects of reality that reporters or scientists often claim to be merely describing. Facts produced and distributed through the media play a large role in our public life. They do not merely provide a mirror on the world; they actively attempt to provide an agenda for what *should be thought about.* Facts disseminated in this way become representations through which our social reality is described, interpreted, criticized, manipulated, distorted, promoted, and discussed – in a word, constructed. To view any set of facts merely as facts would be to lose sight of how the contexts in which they are produced and consumed laden them with meaning and value.

It is worth noting that reporting styles, especially in the media of Western Europe and North America, have evolved away from a stress on the facts to a greater stressing of the methods used to gather the facts. This is particularly evident with investigative or in-depth coverage for television, where methods such as the gathering of supplementary evidence, the presenting of conflicting truth claims, and the liberal use of actual quotations are graphically demonstrated in the presentations.

This stress on the methods of news gathering has helped to establish the authority of the media as "good brokers," but we are still a long way from understanding how people actually interpret and use what is reported to them. What people get out of the representations presented to them will probably have a great deal to do with both their past experience and their present context. Thus, a union worker may well view a strike slogan presented through the media differently than other members of society – perhaps quite differently from those who do the reporting. It is all too easy to mistake what we see in a representation for what others get out of it. This error of attributing to others the meaning we ourselves get out of things is sometimes seen as an example of *representational fallacy*. Representational fallacies are also the result of mistaking the representations for the total environment in which interpretations are made.

15.3.2 Representations as Symbols

"The picture is not a fact but a symbol," a former network news producer has said, through which "the real child and its real crying become symbols of all children."[9] Such a conscious use of people as symbols creates images in which people, whether farmers on the Canadian prairie, Amerindians confronting political and cultural problems, or home owners in a flood plain appear not as individuals but as representatives of the "average" farmer, the "average" Indian or the "average" home owner. Such conventions of classification, media analyst Edward J. Epstein believes, work to provide stable images of groups and their behavior. However, when the convention becomes the predominant recipe of newswork, when cameramen, editors, correspondents, and other producers of visual materials habitually come to select the images for future stories on the basis of past ones the process becomes closed, circular, and self-perpetuating. "Stable images," in such circumstances, can become little more than stereotypes; and their use in the media may do little more than reinforce similar stereotypes already present in the social environment.

15.3.3 Events as Symbols

Events themselves can become symbols. This is especially true of the ceremonies that surround investiture of new governments, official visits by heads of state, or the highly mannered actions which guide courtrooms or religious ceremony. Events of this sort serve principally as a way of maintaining the legitimacy of current political, legal, or religious orders. As symbols, such events resemble and promote the very "legitimacy" they describe. They are representations of the prevailing order and they are representations which promote the prevailing order.

Such events of course carry instructional potential; and they can be manipulative as well. *Pseudo-events* may not be the best term for their manipulative uses, but historian Daniel J. Boorstin has coined the term to describe how both the media and in turn the public can be victimized by them.[10] Pseudo-events are events planned or staged for the purpose of being reported. As such they have an ambiguous relationship to reality and, frequently, they involve a "self-fulfilling prophecy."[11]

A former director of CBS News, Fred Friendly has described how in the 1950s Senator Joseph McCarthy was able to fuel public hysteria simply by declaring that he had evidence of communists working in various departments of government.[12] Typically, McCarthy's announcements were made late in the day, in time for the evening news, but not in time for the reporters responsible to "check out" his claims. It was of course a "fact" that he said such things. But the "facts" were in every case later revealed to be little more than a tissue of lies, spun for the purpose of creating a situation of crisis merely by identifying one. Reporters, although they generally knew what McCarthy was doing, for a time were unwilling or helpless to do anything much about it.

Heinrich Böll, winner of the 1972 Nobel Prize for literature, spoke out about a similar situation in more recent times fueled by the reporting of the nationally distributed German daily *Die Bild* on acts of terrorism allegedly committed by a former television journalist, Ulrike Meinhof. "Where the police are still investigating, making assumptions, conjecturing, *Bild* is already further down the road," Böll wrote of their almost daily linking of all manner of terrorist activity in Germany directly to Meinhof and her "gang." After her capture, Böll publicly called for her official safe conduct out of Germany, "to protect her from the 60 million Germans now hunting witches as they once hunted jews."[13] In North America during this same period, many people noted the irony of the Patty Hearst case, whose grandfather, Randolf Hearst, is largely credited with developing the very sensationalist news formulas to which his granddaughter was subjected by some of the media. All three cases support Boorstin's contention that pseudo-events, by identifying states of crisis, help to create them.

15.4 Conclusion

This last chapter and especially the latter matters addressed in it have brought us full circle, from the task of gaining access to the conceptual world of others to the question of how our modern institutions compound the process of representation itself. By their critical tone, many of the observations in this chapter suggest that we may need to reexamine some of our assumptions about the role of public communication. This may, in fact, become urgent as newer means of communication begin to press upon the borders of cultures and ways of life everywhere.

The next few chapters take up the issue that our analysis of bias has brought us to: the role of the modern institutions of communication themselves and their uses – actual and potential – for public judgment and public action. This we could say is the task of facilitating conversation on a grand scale.

PART FIVE

The Production of Culture

Conflicting versions of social life are part of a process of working out new meanings, values and human practices. As we have seen, institutions and organizations of all sorts play an important part in this process. The chapters to follow look at the means of communication, especially how those means are organized by modern communication institutions, and their role as producers of social reality. The role of the media as a producer of reality is discussed in relation to the public, to social development, and in relation to culture. The emphasis in these chapters lies less on the system of meanings and values and more upon the *structures* (political, economic, and cultural) through which our codes and modes are enacted.

CHAPTER 16

Media and the Public

16.1 The Modern Public

16.1.1 The Ideal Community – Dewey

The concept of the media as secondary mode for the production of culture originated with the interactionist perspective of the Chicago School. Much as George Herbert Mead had stressed the reflexive capacity of language in stabilizing our social reality, his contemporary at the University of Chicago, John Dewey, has pointed to the ways in which the rise of new technologies of communication could destabilize that reality.[1] The new technologies, it appeared to Dewey, moved people away from the shared experiences of community, where knowledge and meaning grew directly out of face-to-face encounters, while at the same time making it possible for citizens to form an acquaintance with broader sorts of experience and interdependence. Older media, like the newspaper, had created a *reading public* of businessmen and neighborhood groupings, concerned with community life. These localized publics, Dewey's colleague Robert Ezra Park observed, came into being specifically to discuss the news.[2] As such, the function of the press began by serving and largely remained rooted to these intersubjective realities of community-centered life.

The rise of an urban industrial society in the twentieth century, including a technological revolution in the means of transportation, brought about changes in the community-centered public. Newer forms of media, such as wire services, nationally distributed magazines, radio networks, and later television began to systematically draw attention away from community orientations, eroding its interpersonal character. In its place a new sort of public began to replace the older one. The newly industrialized and urbanized society that developed in the twentieth century in North America created new and special problems. The newer means of communication seemed more capable of assuming the role of providing the citizenry on a national scale with the news and information it needed to make rational decisions – and in this way to generate a shared sense of social meaning and purpose. The ideal of community, identified in the thought of Mead, Dewey, Park, and other members of the Chicago School, seemed to provide reassurance about this transformation from a locally based public toward a national constituency. If newer communication technologies seemed to assist the erosion of community, it was also possible to see its role in creating another larger public alongside industry and government where the rational discourse of citizens could flourish.

16.1.2 The Role of Media

From these beginnings in the United States the study of the public as something in part created by and maintained by the mass media became an important political theme. In the early decades of the century the work of social scientists seemed to coincide with a perceived need to provide this emerging national public with more rational forms of information on which to base its decisions. Methods used to gather and disseminate information drew upon and fostered communication research techniques. The news emphasized its objective organization and presentation of the "facts," and social scientists of the communication process developed more sophisticated assessments of public opinion through sampling and audience research tools. Even controversial uses of media – for propaganda, for example – were dissected by political analysts with the calm assurance that, once thoroughly analyzed and publicly understood, such uses would wither away into ineffectiveness.

Somewhat ironically, the efforts of this mainstream of research to clarify the conditions and the means by which the media could become more effective (more rational rather than simply more persuasive) resulted in something like a demonstration of the opposite. Paul Lazarsfeld, a pioneer in audience research, saw this when, as early as 1944, he and his colleagues found that the effects of the mass media were slight. "People appeared to be much more influenced in their political decisions by face-to-face contact," they reported, "than by the mass media directly."[3] In the following decades other research underscored their conclusion – that media most effectively serve to strengthen dispositions (attitudes, beliefs, and opinion) already arrived at. And these dispositions, it was suggested, were usually the result of other social, economic, and cultural relationships, all more powerful and persuasive than the media.[4]

However, the recognition of the media as an ineffective organizer of the public led other social scientists to wonder whether the mass media might not actively function to decrease the organization of the public, to privatize the domain of the public itself and, simultaneously, to restrict the public's ability to engage in rational thought and judgments by limiting rather than broadening its agenda. Such a thesis suggests that the mass media may be effective, but in more negative ways than earlier studies suspected. Two of these theses have suggested that the mass media have served to weaken the public through the *decontextualization of public information* and through *deverbalization of public life.*

16.1.3 Decontextualization – Gouldner

Two matters, Alvin Gouldner argues, undermined the initial hopes of the Chicago School for a public stimulated by news and grounded in rational discussion.[5] On the one hand, the Chicago scholars failed to see adequately the self-interests of advertisers, owners, and other social institutions (including governments at all levels) in managing and manipulating news producing organizations toward different ends. The interest in management of news accounts by reporters and other newsworkers has become a pervasive fact of modern media. The news producing system is thus constrained by a *news withholding* or *news censoring system,* based as much on secrecy and concealment as upon active manipulation. Such forms of censorship – and the reluctance of the media to talk about it publicly – has resulted in what Gouldner calls the *decontextualizing of information* from the circumstances which produce or occasion it. Public anxiety about what does not get reported as well as what gets reported through protected (informed and concealed) sources can serve to heighten suspicion and decrease confidence in the news as a basis for reasonable discussion.

On the other hand, this internal censoring of the news-producing system has had a further impact upon the public. Media, as has been pointed out by a range of researchers, differ from oral or face-to-face communication in that the capacity of the media to monitor feedback is severely limited. People in face-to-face situations can utilize what Gregory Bateson called the report and the command aspects of communication (see chapter 10). In interpersonal relations people are able to communicate information and simultaneously to monitor and negotiate their feelings about the communication and toward each other through feedback. Unlike the multimodal possibilities of interpersonal communication, the media can offer only reports. This absence of the command aspect (the feeling or relational context) of communication partially accounts for the limited effectiveness of the media in influencing behavior and judgment. It also suggests why it is that people may regard the reports of the media with distrust (another sort of negative effect.) Furthermore, Gouldner believes, the efforts to counter this by the use of polls, ratings, or even spies, may increase rather than allay public suspicions.

Gouldner, as many others influenced by the ideas and ideals of the Chicago School, remained passionately attached to the importance of the public. His pessimistic assessment of the decline of the public is based in part upon his belief that a weak public makes all democratic processes in a society more difficult. A weakened public generally results in greater secrecy, concealment, and censorship, either the overt state censorship common to Soviet bloc countries or the subtler and more internal forms of censorship we find in the West.

Ironically, Gouldner's analysis seems to suggest that what is not reported may be of as much consequence as what is reported. The message that does not arrive or the parts of the message that are withheld or concealed from us may be an important source of anxiety and cynicism about public life and those who produce it.

16.1.4 Deverbalization – Sennett

Richard Sennett believes the rise of a suspicious public to be a consequence of a wider set of activities than those represented by the mass media.[6] In Sennett's view, the public sphere or domain existed not only as a forum in which to discuss the news, but in its earlier forms, in the eighteenth century especially, as an entire set of rituals of speech and conduct within forms of public architecture that enhanced exchange and discussion with strangers. Sennett sees the decline of the public linked to the disappearance of these conditions and to the appearance in their place of other features of modern society which result in the *deverbalization of public space* – the modern emphasis upon seeing rather than talking and the rise of architectures and styles of social behaviors based upon seeing rather than saying. The elevation of observation over discussion functions to impoverish the multimodal capacities of interpersonal relations. Centralized media similarly provide the citizen with observations, which no matter how skillfully or objectively provided, turn the modern public increasingly toward *spectatorship*.

Both Gouldner and Sennett argue that the style of "objectivity" in use by the modern media may foster suspicion precisely because this style of presenting things seems to withhold information on how the meaning of events is to be understood. In their view, events and opinions presented in an ideological way do not confuse us as to their possible meaning, since they carry their interpretations clearly marked. It is perhaps a measure of our uncertainty in the present century that objectivity and ideology can be regarded from differing points of view as both strategies for knowing and strategies for not knowing – that is both as strategies for revealing and for concealing.

Sennett and Gouldner both provide arguments for why the public and public opinion cannot depend upon the information of the media alone. Their arguments underscore what other researchers have also confirmed – that the formative aspects of publics and their opinions depend strongly upon face-to-face interaction as well. Furthermore, they suggest that it is only at the interpersonal level that alternative sets of values, skills, and arguments (especially values at variance with those of the established media) can emerge directly from interaction and experience. Their arguments have some intriguing parallels with another, more critical, appraisal of the modern public and its problems.

16.2 The Fragmented Public

16.2.1 The Ideal Speech Situation – Habermas

"A part of the public sphere," the sociologist Jürgen Habermas says, "comes into being in every conversation."[7] By stressing *conversation* as the fundamental unit in the formation of the public and its opinions Habermas is building upon the insights of several decades of mass media research which suggest that it is at the community and peer-group level where the formation of opinion crucially occurs. Like the members of the Chicago School, Habermas recognizes speech as the distinctively human capacity and like Robert Ezra Park he acknowledges the particular role played by the early newspapers in bringing into being an active and partisan public to discuss the news.

Unlike the members of the Chicago School, Habermas does not share their optimism that what Dewey called "a great public of human understanding" could follow from the information potentials of the modern technologies of communication. As a German scholar forced to reflect upon the uses of media in his own country during the Nazi period, Habermas is aware of how the control and management of media institutions can generate quite different potentials from those Dewey had in mind. The formation of a more rational public and more rational public opinion, Habermas believes, depends not only upon the type of news and information available but depends as well upon the situations we have available for discussing the meaning and significance of that news or information.

Habermas argues that it is the *interpersonal situation* in which we discuss and converse that provides the necessary and proper context for informed opinion. If that context contains restrictive limitations on who can speak or upon what can be brought into question, or if the context contains violence or the symbolic threat of violence, then the potential for a reasonable discussion is diminished accordingly. For Habermas, the rational formation of the public and its opinion depends upon the conditions of interpersonal life. His concept of an *ideal speech situation* is meant to stress the need for (1) adequate opportunity for people to speak; (2) adequate opportunity to question the rules or the topic of discussion; (3) adequate opportunity to acquire the skills of discourse (including the technical skills of basic media); (4) adequate opportunity to be free from violence and other forms of coercion. Our social institutions either do or do not provide and ensure these conditions. In much the same spirit as did the Chicago School, Habermas suggests that we should analyze, criticize, and, where necessary, modify these institutions according to how effectively they serve and encourage the formation of rational discussion and organization in the aforementioned ways.[8]

16.2.2 A Critique of the Public – the Frankfurt School

Habermas' work is indebted not only to the Chicago School's interest in the public, but it also draws upon the legacy of members of the Frankfurt School, for whom the mass media were an oppressive institution in modern society. The Frankfurt School grew out of the activities of the Institute for Social Research, begun in Germany in 1923 and shifted to the United States in the thirties, where it remained in exile until after the Second World War. The opposition of the Frankfurt Institute to the rise of fascism in Europe, combined with the subsequent difficulties and disagreements its members had with the aims of commercial media in America (which they called producers of mass culture), resulted in a critique of modern media as a consciousness industry willfully manipulating a passive and increasingly irrational public. Two interrelated matters in particular troubled the Frankfurt School about the role of modern media. As victims of European fascism they reacted to the disproportionate influence of media in setting the agenda of *what should be thought about* in society; and, as newly arrived immigrants steeped in a social psychoanalytic tradition of scholarship, they responded sharply to *the way in which* media encouraged people to think about their lives.[9]

In his studies of the content of popular cultural materials Leo Lowenthal found that, especially in the case of popular biographies (perhaps the single most widely read subject matter in the present century), the continuous repetition of the themes of politics, power, and leadership could result in readers falsely accepting the fact that their own lives were the result of social, economic, and political circumstances beyond their personal knowledge or control.[10] What troubled Lowenthal was that the phony facts of such biographies encouraged the feeling in people that they could not hope to understand these realities. This, he believed, promoted passivity and acceptance of the way things are.

Another member of the Frankfurt School Theodor Adorno pointed to the astrology columns of daily newspapers as an example of how the media encourage ways of thinking.[11] Adorno rejected the idea that astrology columns were regarded simply as entertainment by the majority of readers. Astrology columns, he said, were forms of pseudo-rationality. It was pseudo-rationality because it was not based upon social or psychological reality, and because it actively encouraged readers to seek explanations for their particular circumstances in the stars rather than in historical events and real relationships. Whatever their entertainment value, Adorno maintained, such columns discourage people from thinking for themselves or from seeking other forms of advice and counsel. Together, these two theses suggested that *particular forms* of media and *particular contents,* by limiting the agenda of themes and by providing forms of advice without feedback (without reciprocity), encouraged passivity and irrationality.

These latter arguments are strong condemnations of some forms of popular media and, just as much, they are recognitions of the manipulative potentials hidden in seemingly innocuous forms of the language of popular culture. Partly as a consequence of issues raised by these two critical traditions of the Chicago and Frankfurt Schools, some recent attempts have been made to identify these distorting influences of organized communication.

16.2.3 Distorted Communication – Mueller

Claus Mueller defines distorted communication as "forms of restricted and prejudiced communication that by their nature inhibit a full discussion of problems, issues, and ideas that have public relevance." Mueller identifies three principal forms of distorted communication: *directed communication, arrested communication,* and *constrained communication.*[12]

Directed communication results from the efforts of governments to control public communication by attempting to structure the language. Nazi Germany was the archetypal case for such efforts to direct public awareness through language regulation and manipulation. Mueller shows how the Office of the Press continuously strove to control the possible meaning of events by restricting the vocabulary that could be applied to them.

Thus, in 1939 the German Press was advised by the Secretary of the Press that "the word 'war' has to be avoided in all news coverage and editorials. Germany is repulsing a Polish attack"; and in 1941 on the opening of the Eastern Front against the Soviet Union, "There should be no more references to Soviet or Soviet Russian soldiers. At most they can be called Soviet army members or just simply Bolsheviks, beasts, and animals."[13]

The language of public communication in the Germany of that era was characterized by a high frequency of emotive terms, superlatives, and repeated slogans. In this way the normal flexibility of language was controlled through the "frozen content" of public symbols and the widespread use of nouns without qualifying adjectives.

Arrested communication refers to the way in which a limited competency to use language, especially what Mueller calls the official languages of the mass media, schools, and advertising, severely restricts the capacity of individuals and groups to seek and to mobilize the institutional channels and resources of a society for their own needs. Thus, Mueller finds that many people are denied the full resources of such institutions, in part, because they are unable to command the necessary linguistic competency to deal with them.

By contrast, *constrained communication* refers to the active effort of government and business to restrict the flow of information offering differing or embarrassing viewpoints. The cumulative consequence of such forms of censorship or restricted points of view dim the critical capacities of audiences and enhance the possibility of representational fallacies. As Mueller says, "If members of the audience have no counter-interpretations or alternative sources of information, they may mistake for the real world the selected messages presented by the media."[14]

16.3 Conclusion

These arguments are a forceful reminder that many of the representations we receive about our social reality depend upon organized, intentional efforts for their production and dissemination. The public itself may be partly a construction of these various media and the degree of reason or rationality we expect from that public may depend upon the conditions we provide for its organization and the ideas we provide for the formation of its opinions. The Chicago School pointed to the ways in which the new technologies of distribution created a greater equality of readers and hearers. Yet the subsequent observations of the Frankfurt School in Europe and America caution us that it is not what is seen and heard but how it is used that counts. Without an effective public, the ideal of reality-disclosing institutions like the mass media become reality-defining and reality-confining institutions in practice.

The public, Habermas reminds us, comes into being with every conversation. In fact, there seems to be a suggestion in all of this work that the unit of analysis of the public ought to be something like the conversation, something which will help us work toward an understanding of how the public works at the level of interpersonal relations to utilize the media resources and the sorts of discussion available to it. Such a suggestion implies that we need to know more about the public and its conditions than the data of opinion polls and other sampling techniques can give us. The public revealed through sampling is valuable information, but it remains an abstract public. It begins but it does not take us far enough toward understanding how the media can and do animate the interaction of the many publics which make up our collective opinions, judgments, and actions.

CHAPTER 17

The Development Process

17.1 Dependency Theory

17.1.1 The Ideal of Culture – Innis

"Improvements in communication," Harold Innis suggested in the 1950s, can also "make for increased difficulties of understanding."[1] With this central insight Innis became one of the first analysts of the communication process to appreciate the dynamic relationship between the development of communication media and the stability of a culture. As a Canadian, Innis saw clearly the consequences which emerged from the growth of national media systems. In the twentieth century Canada found itself positioned between formidable giants – a declining British empire which had formed Canada's economy and influenced the character of its political institutions, and an expansive American presence, poised to assume the role of principal trading and communication partner.

Innis perceived that centralized systems of mass communication had had significant impact on social organization as well. At the same time as frontier areas were gaining access to the urban centers through the technological transformations of transportation and communication, the urban centers of the continent were also gaining access to remote and previously inaccessible publics. The pattern of development that provided access for peripheries to centers and vice versa did not stop at or respect national boundaries. Especially where common languages provided an easy and economical bridge, centrally organized mass media could draw even peripheral countries more and more into the orbit of larger nation-states. New mass communication technologies provided new forms of social organization and simultaneously reorganized older patterns of interaction at local, regional, even national, levels.

To people at the margins the benefits of access to the informational resources of the larger centers came at the eventual price of greater dependency upon those centers. It was not specific forms of technology that brought this about, but a matter of whether the technology was organized to reflect the interests of centers or peripheries. The printing press, for example, has been both a local and regional resource and, through wire services and chain ownerships, it has also appeared to some to be increasingly an agency of remote control.

Patterns of decentralization and recentralization are always present in a culture. Innis believed they help to shape a culture's dynamics and indicate its overall health. The ideal culture, he proposed, represents a dynamic balance between localizing and centralizing tendencies. By drawing attention to the transformations of social organization that communication technologies could bring about, Innis helped describe the part played by technologies in the process of cultural change; and he helped us see as well why such technologies might be resisted or feared.

Innis was the historical realist who pushed his analysis beyond the technological romanticism of the early Chicago School. Stressing the capacity of communication technology to both *strengthen* and *erode* culture, Innis challenged the conventional wisdom of all those who viewed technology as an inherently progressive step, often without regard for the special interests which promoted and controlled it. By showing how the growth of a domestic mass communication system helped move Canada away from the British sphere of influence only to open it up to reabsorption into a vastly greater American one, Innis was able to demonstrate graphically the trade-offs attached to media development. His concepts of *decentralization* and *recentralization* suggest that communication technologies are far from neutral with regard to matters of culture. In fact, Innis proposed the concept of *cultural monopoly* to emphasize those extremes of imbalance which are created when particular groups or particular nations come to dominate the principal media of communication. Such monopolies Innis believed to be inherently unstable forms. Their presence, he said, leads inevitably to the erosion and collapse of previously viable forms of cultural expression. The progressive view that the improved channels of communication provided by technological innovation automatically lead to improved understanding seems to result from something like a bias in favor of technology. What we learn from Innis is that such a bias overlooks the way in which technologies are always organized around some set of interests. Not infrequently those interests and the interests of a particular culture may result in conflict.[2]

17.1.2 Cultural Inequality

In more recent times countries of the so-called "third world" or "southern tier" have voiced concern over similar problems inherent in the relationships of centers to peripheries. Much as Innis characterized the dynamics of media as a process of decentralization and recentralization, Third World countries have remarked on how the creation of their own national radio and television systems resulted in broadcasting systems which remained to a great extent dependent upon the developed countries (especially the United States) both for models of organization and for the programs themselves. Through forums of research and debate such as UNESCO and, more reluctantly, through the development agencies in the developed countries, a sense of urgency about these issues has emerged. In countries which had passed through intensive periods of decolonization and struggles for greater political autonomy, the newly developed media systems, partly because of their dependence upon the industrialized nations for cheap programming, seemed to resemble agencies of *recolonization.* Along with this criticism has come the realization that the role the media had been found to play in industrialized countries could not be automatically reproduced in other countries with profoundly different histories, cultures, and paths of development. The slow and hesitant recognition of these problems may have been due in part to the fact that the expertise on which media development in the Third World had been based came originally from the experiences and the expectations of the industrialized world itself.[3]

Armand Mattelart has called this a consequence of the *law of unequal exchange.*[4] Experts who encouraged media development in the Third World on the basis of their knowledge of industrialized societies tended to overlook the observations and complaints of indigenous critics living within those developing areas. The circumstance Mattelart points to is a complex matter. The dominant experience on which communication experts have based themselves has been that of the United States, the dominant language in which the research of experts is written remains the English language and, of course, the dominant source of media organization and programming has been, by and large, American. Recent research in the West has begun to acknowledge the impact of these disproportions upon others, even, in fact, upon the many cultural minorities contained within the Western countries themselves. Much as Innis does, these recent research results stress that imbalance and instability result not only from the disproportion in trade and communication, but from the failure of larger countries to acknowledge the feedback from their smaller partners.[5]

It is the failure of corrective feedback through channels which would allow peripheries and minorities to be acknowledged at the centers and with the majorities that seems to have led a variety of nations, regions, and even ethnic and cultural groups to begin to question the wisdom of the central principle of international mass communication – *the free flow of information.* In brief the principle of free flow is a statement of professed faith on the part of many countries in the human right to express and to disseminate information without unnecessary censorship or barriers, including the barriers created by ideological differences and reinforced by the power of governments to inhibit such flows. It is also an indirect expression of the right of people to receive information, although this part of the principle, especially as stated by the United Nations, remains rather ambiguous. Numerous criticisms have been mounted to demonstrate how the mass media of larger economic and political systems are more capable of taking advantage of such a principle than others. Few of these critics and fewer nations question the "principle" of the free flow of information. What is questioned instead is the predominantly one-way flow of information. Much as Harold Innis' work did for an earlier period, such challenges seem to call upon us to reexamine our ideals and our assumptions about the media against the historical record itself.[6]

One set of suggestions that has come forward calls for more attention to be paid to developing genuine forms of reciprocity between center and margins, beginning with an effort to make centers and margins more aware and accountable to each other's needs. At the same time, many countries of the peripheries have become aware that center-periphery communication flows (even more reciprocal flows) may need to be offset by greater efforts at establishing communication among peripheries themselves, especially where problems and interests are held in common. In fact, some countries have already recognized the mutual interests and mutual problems that exist between countries and peoples on the peripheries. The concepts of reciprocity and mutuality may well become significant tools in the rethinking of information and communication flows that has already begun.

17.2 Social Interaction Theory

17.2.1 Communication and Community – Felstehausen

The demand for mass media in the Third World arose not only from the availability of the technology and from the ambitions of nationalism but from the development of social reform policies in countries which required new mechanisms for the diffusion of new knowledge and work techniques. Mass media modes held out the promise of quick and efficient solutions to the age-old problems imposed by difficult terrain and illiteracy. Film, radio, and television all seemed able to overcome the isolation of backlands and the limitations of oral cultures. But, within the decision to use the media for disseminating information, especially information related to health and agriculture, were hidden assumptions, many untested and many more simply inappropriate to the actual circumstances of the Third World.

In hindsight much of what we now know about the limitations of media has resulted from the open assessments of the failure of these efforts on the part of their original promoters and researchers. We now know, for instance, that communication cannot be equated with *information exchange*;[7] we know that communication is not an *independent variable* and does not, by itself, result in attitude change, let alone in changes of behavior;[8] and we know with certainty that the impact of communication upon development and social change cannot be studied, even as an *intervening variable,* without reference to the social, economic, and political circumstances operating at the time.[9] Yet, erroneous and untried assumptions were part of what was exported, along with the basic technology of mass media, to the developing countries. The rejection of these assumptions represents another stage in the rethinking of media that has fed back to us from those Third World experiences.

As part of this reevaluation, Herman Felstehausen has proposed the concept of the communication community as the proper unit of analysis for information processes which involve the mass media.[10] The concept of community in communication analyses, he believes, ought to be equivalent to the firm in business analyses; as a concept it emphasizes rather than ignores the concrete interrelationship of communication processes with the social structure: "the concept of community provides the scope needed to take account of rules, sanctions, status, power, economic motives, customs, beliefs, values, and rituals." Felstehausen's own studies provide evidence for what happens when the realities of community structure are overlooked.

In the late sixties, government agencies in the State of Antioquia in Colombia tried to stem the flow of people to the urban centers by initiating information campaigns to inform local community leaders about services available to them for planning local improvements. Felstehausen monitored the responses of several communities to one improvement option – that of road construction – for two years. During that time and in spite of the information campaign no road construction was undertaken by the local government. In fact, the road construction which did occur resulted from the private efforts of local groups which skirted community leaders and the local government entirely. Persons in established positions of control in communities, Felstehausen concluded, often resist efforts to alter the rules of the game.

The role communication plays seems to be defined by the particular community structure and not the other way around, as media developers tended to believe. The message in this sense is what the community makes of it. The sense that is made out of media-imparted information by a community cannot be described without a clear sense of the structure of communication and power within that community. *Information,* Felstehausen says, refers only to the message content which is shifted around in the communication process, but *communication* refers to "the social, organizational, and psychological dynamics of human message transmission and reception – that is, the processes which describe information flows as well as their effects on senders and receivers and the processes whereby meanings themselves are changed."[11] Communication is not about the transmission of changes in attitudes and behaviors; it is about the transformation of the "messages" themselves in the process of being transmitted, exchanged, shared, and otherwise moved around.

17.2.2 Communication and Intelligibility – Hymes

The process by which people integrate and make sense of information within communities is sometimes referred to as *mutual intelligibility*. The process of mutual intelligibility always occurs within and between what the ethnographer Dell Hymes calls speech communities.[12] Speech communities are comprised of various repertoires or ways of speaking – not just language, but norms of interaction and conduct in conversations as well as attitudes toward identity and status. It is these features of the speech community that determine how material of the media will be constructed and transformed into meanings. School children, for instance, who appear to resist speaking the standard versions of English they witness through media, or even the teacher's version, can sometimes be observed talking "that way" when playing school or playing out television roles. Speech communities can be forceful ways of constraining other influences, such as the talk of television and teachers, without otherwise prohibiting such contacts. Like ways of seeing referred to in earlier chapters, ways of speaking have the force of a bias.

Within speech communities the media are part of the ways of speaking and communicating in that community. Ways of speaking, for the most part, are not extensions of the media. Hymes believes "it entirely possible that a medium may have a constitutive effect in one community and not in another due to its qualitative role, its social meaning and function, even though frequencies of occurrence may be the same in both."[13] By *constitutive effect* Hymes refers to the way speech communities actually transform the information they receive from the media. Early media experts assumed that the various mass media entered into different sections of society, different cultures, and different groups and communities in more or less similar ways. Early development schemes in the Third World faithfully reflected this belief in the animating power of the newer media, to reach everybody in the same way at some basic level. Subsequent questions about the constitutive function of media information in individual communities have shifted our concerns from general notions about the means of informing to more detailed investigations of the meaning of received communication in actual communities.

Ethnographies of this sort represent a challenge to one of the most persistant ideas behind media development, what might be called the myth of the media as *transformers of reality*. Those who embrace notions of mass media as transformers of social reality are not wrong in their respect for the potential of information technologies. Their failure may be, in fact, a result of their emphasis on the *means of transmission* rather than the *transformation of meaning*. To understand the transformation of information-meaning requires precise observation inside the communities themselves. By failing to respect the diversity of the speech communities which make use of the information provided and by failing to take account of the differences which exist among communities of communicators, many development theorists and specialists have been tacitly promoting a transmission model for instruction and learning in the Third World that had already been brought into question through thinkers such as Dewey and Innis closer to home.

Dewey and Innis both accepted aspects of the transmission model of communication, but each had begun to recognize the significant diversities and differences within and among cultures and communities and, like the ethnographers, they were looking for a fuller appreciation of the complexities and inequities among people. In fact, the *inequality among cultures,* which Innis saw tied to the uses of media, has been provided with strong ethnographic support through Hymes identification of the inequalities among speakers. Hymes notes four ways in which communication communities can produce inequalities: (1) in the adaptive resources of the spoken language itself (languages are not all equally flexible); (2) in terms of the different personal competencies found in a community and the influence of personality on those competencies; (3) according to the various institutions of the community (especially their role in fostering verbal skills and resources); and (4) by the values and beliefs of a community at a particular time.[14]

It is insufficient to equate information with knowledge or power and to deal as many early development experts did only with the problem of providing access. Access to information is not enough by itself. Access to information does not overcome the *structural differences* which the dependency theorists describe in detail. Access to information does not overcome the *functional differences* in language use nor the differences in ability within and among communities, cultures, and social groups. "Every speech community," Hymes says, "is to some degree caught up in a changing relationship with a larger context, in which opportunities for the meaningful use of traditionally fostered abilities may be declining, and novel opportunities (or requirements) for which members have not been traditionally prepared may be impinging."[15]

Communication communities are always characterized by

differential abilities and *opportunities*. When we fail to recognize these differentials we may do so in the progressive belief that all of us have potentially the same relative capabilities. Early media development theorists emphasized this and it would seem that the uses of media in the Third World for social reform were based upon similar assumptions.

What sensitive scholars such as Felstehausen and Hymes suggest is that an analysis of the uses of information within actual communities reveals a startlingly complex reality. By stressing the differential abilities and opportunities which characterize the process of sense-making within actual communities, Felstehausen and Hymes make a persuasive case that it is the patterns and conditions of social interaction that shape and constitute the consequences of access to information more surely than the information or the access itself.

17.3 Conclusion

The concepts of mutual intelligibility and community help us to grasp the process by which information comes to have the meaning placed upon it that it does. For those concerned with social interaction this sense-making process can be revealed only by careful attention to the actual ways of communicating within and among communities and with due respect for their differences. Stressing the diversity of communities helps to make more explicit the way in which social meaning depends upon that interplay of linguistic, personal, institutional, and ideological features which we previously referred to as characterizing the *intersubjective context*. Together they indicate something of the complex social role of information, an issue already of international concern.

CHAPTER 18

Culture and Social Meaning

18.1 Cultural Formation – Williams

18.1.1 The Ideal of Cultural Democracy

The arguments from the previous chapter that we need to look more deeply into the actual empirical world of communicators, arguments indebted to the experiences of the Third World and also to the work of ethnographers, have a counterpart amongst those who study the formation of culture in industrialized countries. These theorists of modern culture believe we face something like a crisis today in our organized communication systems. The British cultural historian Raymond Williams describes it as a crisis brought on "by the speed of invention and by the difficulty of finding the right institutions in which these technical means are to be used."[1] On the one hand, the new media have not lived up to the high hopes once entertained for their use; on the other hand, their systematic abuse – for propaganda, for commercial profit, and for efforts to manage democracy rather than to extend it – has served to actively undermine that potential.

Thus far in the present century, media development has been largely a result of our political and economic initiatives. Because of this Williams believes we have slipped into viewing modern communication media as merely an epiphenomena of politics and business, that is, as a method of government or as a means of trade; and consequently, we now tend to see the uses of media as a choice between institutions controlled by state monopolies or by private commercial interests. The result is a vicious circle. Our views of the media are shaped by the assumptions we hold about the communication process and its role in society; and these assumptions, in turn, are embodied in the practices of actual media institutions, which disseminate the very assumptions on which they are based. For Williams the current communication media are simply an extension of these older political and economic models and assumptions; and the crisis that has been produced is a cultural crisis precisely because it is the cultural role of media that has been neglected in favor of its political and economic functions.

To see what is meant by the cultural role of media it is necessary to grasp how Williams sees institutions mediating social interaction. Williams believes that the communication institutions we have produced in the twentieth century are based upon four models or ideals: (1) the authoritarian, (2) the paternal, (3) the commercial, and (4) the democratic. The problems stemming from these models in actual use are considerable. The *authoritarian model,* for example, creates a powerful apparatus of state intervention and control. The media system of the German Third Reich is the classic example. Ironically, Williams points out that the propaganda network employed by the Nazis was one of the only systems to bring radio use within the literal definition of mass communication. This was done through Party organization of compulsory public listening sessions and the installation of receivers in the streets. Less ironically, the type of communication organization set up under authoritarian regimes of this sort operate for the purpose of perpetuating the power of the ruling minority. Contrary opinion is not tolerated, and so retreats underground.

The *paternalistic model* of communication describes institutional situations where content is dictated in a benevolent manner by a ruling minority who believe that their definition of culture, while perhaps not the only one, is certainly the more beneficial. What is asserted by paternalistic institutions is the duty to protect and guide "the masses." Protection, in this sense, takes the form of direct censorship of distasteful opinion or deliberate exclusion of damaging opinion. Though the purpose remains the same as with more authoritarian arrangements, there is no direct coercion involved and attempts are made to "justify" things as they are. As examples of paternalistic institutions Williams mentions the British Broadcasting Corporation, as well as the more tightly controlled state television systems in France and Italy.[2]

The *commercial model* of communication is defined, at least partly, by opposition to the authoritarian and the paternal forms. Although such systems seem to provide a good deal of freedom of communication through the marketplace, the actual historical development of commercial media reveals a pattern of very *uneven competition.* Especially in the case of the press and television, uneven competition results from the disproportion between large-scale networks and small-scale community stations, or between international chains and local independent presses. Production costs and production facilities often severely limit the relative degrees of freedom and access within such overall arrangements. As Williams says, "the control claimed as a matter of *power* by authoritarians, and as a matter of *principle* by paternalists, is often achieved as a matter of *practice* in the operation of the commercial system. Anything can be said, provided that you can say it and that you can say it profitably."[3]

By contrast, Williams sees a *democratic model* of communication arising out of the need for an *improved institutional framework* for our present and future technological means of communication. Williams' democratic model is really a formula for restructuring existing communication institutions. Just what Williams means by the democratic model is, in part, his critical response to the failures of both the paternal and the commercial practices of our present media. In the former case, paternalist practices demonstrate the dangers of allowing a few to control access to the media, thereby limiting the freedom of expression in favor of an elite. While in the latter case, commercial practices demonstrate the dangers of a media which does not have to be responsible to anyone other than private financial groups for what it does, does not have to answer public criticism directly and does not have to permit, let alone encourage, a relationship between those who contribute the media's content and the public it reaches and serves.

Where present institutions of media invariably fail, Williams believes, is in their inability to serve the cultural needs of society. The cultural needs of a society cannot be adequately served by commercial institutions alone because, he argues, this produces little more than a commercial culture. And they cannot be served much better by paternalistic institutions created by governments because this leads to an elite culture which fails to represent the diversity of cultural practices or, worse, leads to an official culture which fails to understand the process of learning and expressing through which reality is continuously formed and changed.

Much as Innis had earlier, Williams looks at the balancing of major interests in a society – political, economic, and cultural – as an indication of its overall health. The ideal of a democratic culture grows out of his belief that communication institutions can be restructured to exploit the potential for universal accessibility to learning and to democracy. Audiences created by electronic media and the abundance of inexpensive publications provide a means to this end. But while technologies, present and proposed, offer the potential for an educated and participating citizenry, the existing uses of communication technologies prevent the realization of this potential. Like Innis, Williams has also documented the way in which the democratic potential of the media often has been weakened through control by powerful minorities, what he calls "hegemony."[4]

18.1.2 Dominant and Emergent Influences

Cultural hegemony refers to the dominant features of thought within a social order, to the way in which general conceptions of reality are diffused through institutions and serve to inform the values, principles, and social relations of its citizenry. *Hegemonic culture* refers to the fact that in actual societies there exist inequalities which prevent some people from participating in this process as freely or as completely and influentially as others. Thus all cultures are characterized by groups with disproportionate influence and, through their control of media organizations, all cultures are suffused with a correspondingly disproportionate influence of certain types of values, conventions, and human practices.

The existence of dominant and subordinate relations has been a recurring theme in those writers concerned with the way cultures are produced and preserved. Much of the critical response from the Third World has been a response to what they perceive as the hegemonic content and style of media products; and Innis also made such hegemonic relations a central matter through his concept of cultural monopolies. Biographically, Williams shares a similar perspective. As a native of rural Wales, he saw first hand the way relations between the colonizing first world and the colonized Third World were mirrored in Great Britain through rural and industrial ways of life, in the tension between the country and the city, and in the way cultural codes in his own society seemed to favor the dominant urban industrial elites, their values, and ideas.[5]

What distinguishes Williams' work in communications and culture is his grasp of the fact that hegemonic processes are not only *formative* features of culture but *transformative* as well. "The reality of any hegemony," he maintains, "is that, while by definition it is always dominant, it is never either total or exclusive."[6] Thus, at any time, alternative or oppositional forms of culture and politics also exist in a society. *Counter-hegemony* and *alternative-hegemony* are Williams' way of identifying the forms of resistance, sources for alternative action, and challenges to thought and convention that occur outside or at the edge of the dominant practices.

Through alternative responses in a culture it is possible to see not only the adaptive and incorporating features of the cultural process, but also from where the significant transformations and authentic breaks with the dominant features of a culture can come. These latter features Williams believes to be part of the democratic impulses of a culture and often the source of its creative and critical expression. The dominant features of culture are usually those which refer to completed situations, to fully articulated beliefs, conventions, and forms of life. Most conventional human practices, as well as much art and literature, belong here – to the *manifest* social and cultural formations.

By contrast, *emergent* formations characterize situations that are incomplete, still in process and, at such stages, usually reflect peripheral or minority interests.[7] Art, literature, and politics are frequently the modes in which such emergent formations appear and through which counter and oppositional activity can be first identified. Such emergent formations form the leading edge of new social meanings, providing meanings which can be understood by others but which have not yet become a part of the general beliefs and conventions of a culture. Williams calls this sharing of new meanings a structure of feeling. *Structures of feeling* identify a process in which new contributions, especially in the arts, politics, and morality, find receptivity in sections of the public which are able to make sense of these new expressions in terms of their own experience. Structures of feeling, as well as counter and alternative hegemonies and emergent formations, all point to the complex error we commonly make when we think the role of communication institutions can be, or is, limited simply to the transmission of dominance. Two other concepts, those of ideology and ritual, help to expand and deepen our understanding of what is meant by the *formative processes* of culture and social meaning.

18.2 The Role of Ideology – Geertz

"Ideologies," cultural anthropologist Clifford Geertz says, "are, most distinctively, maps of problematic social reality and matrices for the creation of collective conscience." Ideologies are often regarded as politicized accounts of social reality, full of figurative and colorful imagery and held with fervor and intensity by those who have accepted them. Such definitions of ideology are by and large critical, even pejorative accounts of ideology, which regard the function of ideologies as a mask by which some people conspire to seek power or as a remedy by which others attempt to escape anxiety. Ideologies, we are frequently told, are matters we could well do without. The Nazi ideology or the beliefs of religious sects such as the Moonies or Jonestowners are often used to point up the extremes of the case; but just as inquisitions or the burning of witches does not invalidate all forms of religion, neither does it typify them. Hostile views of ideology, Geertz says, fail to understand the deeper function that ideology serves.[8]

Whether we approve or disapprove, ideologies function to give meaning to otherwise incomprehensible social situations and they do so in ways which make possible some sort of purposive action on the part of those who adopt them. In fact, ideologies seem to emerge as authoritative concepts at precisely those points where our notions of conventional morality, our normal political practices, or our unquestioned economic recipes seem no longer adequate. Formal ideologies arise, according to Geertz, when the traditional strategies in a culture or society either "trammel political behavior by encumbering it with transcendental significance, or stifle political imagination by binding it to the blank realism of habitual judgment."[9]

Ideologies are the result of a complex social-symbolic process Geertz calls *patterns of interworking meaning.* Ideologies draw significantly upon symbolic resources in transforming what begin as personal attitudes into what ultimately become public forms of action. As a case in point, Geertz describes the controversy which surrounded the introduction of the Taft-Hartley Labor Act in the United States after World War II. In their opposition to a number of provisions in the act, labor organizations branded the legislation as a "slave labor law." In the campaign that followed (one which incidentally failed), labor unions attempted to arouse their members, to solicit public support, and to lobby legislators into opposing the passage of the act. The phrase "slave labor law" is, of course, an ideological one. What is troublesome about it, Geertz finds, is not its imagery, but the way in which the use of such symbols is frequently viewed as an example of distortion, oversimplification, or provocation. To so so, Geertz believes, is to mistake the *manifest* or literal content of such a label for the deeper and more complex meanings such a symbol has for those employing it. To overlook the deeper meanings of such a slogan is also, arguably, to indirectly disparage the thought processes of a great many intelligent supporters of the underlying issues. No one after all actually believed the Taft-Hartley Act would reduce workers to the status of slaves. Geertz points out that such metaphors derive their power from the interworking of a "multiplicity of referential connections between it and social reality." The power of ideology, and its role in the formation of social meaning, lies in "its capacity to grasp, formulate, and communicate social realities" that have eluded conventional efforts to do so. Ideologies here closely resemble Williams' structure of feeling in that they produce social meanings that others can relate to their own individual experience.

18.3 The Role of Rituals – Carey's Example of Death

In his extension and elaboration of the work of Geertz and Williams, James Carey has proposed the following example.[10] Imagine a conversation on the meaning of death. One participant, a physician, proposes that death occurs on the cessation of brain waves. Another, a typical North American, argues that death occurs on the cessation not of the brain but the heart. Yet another, an Irish peasant, insists that death occurs only three days after the cessation of the heart. The final participant, a member of the Ik tribe, a mountain people of Uganda, maintains that death occurs seven days prior to the cessation of the heartbeat. Each of course has reasons for his position and each position in turn contains meaningful connections to the social reality in question. The physician's argument draws upon clinical science and preserves an interest in the suffering of the patient. The typical North American draws upon the cultural associations with the heart and, therefore, preserves in his judgment an interest also in the feelings of the "survivors" of the deceased. On the other hand, the Irish peasant draws upon the traditional rites of passage – the wake and celebration – through which the final separation and accounting by the community is preserved. And finally, the Ik tribesman draws upon the ethos of survival, by which the integrity of the tribe is preserved and not unnecessarily threatened when a member of the tribe is no longer able to fend for and feed himself.

Is it possible, Carey asks, to choose amongst these definitions, into which enter aspects of science, sentiment, religious custom, and material circumstance? How, in fact, could we account for their differences? Not, Carey suggests, by an appeal to any one set of formal explanations. "What men create is not just one reality," he says, "but multiple realities."[11] Consequently no one symbolic form – art, science, ideology, religion, or mythology – can adequately tap such complex and diverse formulations. We may, of course, see that certain societies favor certain of these symbolic forms in their explanations and definitions, but for the most part our modern cultures are a mélange of these symbolic forms or recipes. Carey calls this defining and constraining role of symbolic forms the signifying practices of communication. These signifying practices – scientific, artistic, religious, political – are the maps, templates, and blinders through which we encounter and make meaningful sense of our world. Like Geertz' ideology, Carey's signifying practices of science, religion, and survival constitute modes through which we actively formulate the social meanings of a culture.

Carey's example should have special significance for us if we bear in mind that our various forms of sense-making are also ways in which we promote particular attitudes, values, and types of behavior over others. His example underscores the importance of recognizing the ritual function of all symbol systems, including our own.

18.4 Conclusion

What may at first seem to be an unlikely union of materials in this chapter all share a common concern for the formation and maintenance of meaning within a culture. Through widely differing points of view, Williams, Geertz, and Carey all look beyond the manifest surface of cultural life and meaning to the conditions that lie behind our forms and recipes for producing the meanings that make up our social and cultural order. To move beyond the surface and to push deeper into the empirical reality of meaning requires attention to the complex ways in which such systems of meanings and the conditions underlying them mediate – that is define, enable, and constrain – all our human practices.

For Williams, democracy is not only a form of political activity, but an irreducible feature of cultural life, best illustrated by the way in which emergent forms of expression produce new meanings at the margins of – and sometimes in conflict with – the dominant forms of thought and behavior. Geertz points to ideologies in much the same spirit. Since ideologies seem to arise at points where conventional sense-making and conventional actions seem unpromising, it would be unwise to see them simply as forms of deception or provocation. Such an attitude takes too superficial a view of the public formation of public symbols, and too ungenerous a view of other people's thoughts and motives. The world in which we take up residence, Carey reminds us, is one that we continuously construct through a variety of beliefs, conventions, and human practices, but all of which conform to those signifying practices that make up the centers and the margins of a culture.

The final chapters offer a summary, both intellectual and practical, and some suggestions about the choice of appropriate units of analysis for understanding the communication process. The question of appropriate units of analysis is an unavoidable one, if only because the knowledge we produce through the units of analysis we choose will have consequences for the world we investigate.

PART SIX

Principles and Practices

Perhaps the most far-reaching issue involving communication is the question of why some versions of reality come to hold significance for us and others do not. We have, of course, a number of pat answers for this: it's a result of socialization, of material circumstance, even the result of accident and deliberate choice. All of these, in a sense, are reasonable accounts. Yet, all are more descriptions of the outcome than they are explanations that help us understand the process.

The account proposed in the following chapters is only a partial one, but it recapitulates an argument that extends throughout the text. It is essentially this: that while socialization, material circumstance, accident, and choice are significant ways of accounting for the production of reality, so too are the modes, codes, and technological means of communication *through which* and *in which* reality is ordered, defined, disseminated, and constrained – its signifying web.

CHAPTER 19

The Legitimation process

19.1 Institutional Orders – Berger and Luckmann

19.1.1 Types of Legitimation

All institutional orders are continuously constructed, explained, and justified. Moreover, all institutional orders must be transmitted from one generation to another. Each new generation, sociologists Peter L. Berger and Thomas Luckmann note, poses the problem of compliance, for what the previous generation may have experienced first hand a new generation gets largely as hearsay. If only for this reason, every modern institutional order must rely in part upon its modes, codes, and technological means of communication to legitimate itself from one generation to another.

Legitimations of the social order are present in virtually all forms of communication in society. Berger and Luckmann identify four basic ways in which this occurs.[1] *Incipient legitimation* refers to the explanations that are built into the vocabulary of everyday life. By supplying names, such as "wife" or "policeman," the language conveys information that also prescribes modes of conduct which are learned along with the name itself. The naming of reality, at this level, also provides commonsense explanations about our relationship to it.

Explanatory schemes constitute a second type of legitimation.

Here, basic justifications are embodied in common maxims and proverbs and the bits of folk wisdom which continue to offer insight into the nature of a particular institutional order. A third type consists of *explicit theories.* Depending upon the diversity and complexity of the society, such theories can range from elaborate explanations of kinship systems by elders of a clan to the sorts of "sciences" of kinship which have developed in our present century and which have no clear relationship to the situations they describe. In the latter case, anthropology, for instance, has been somewhat unfairly characterized as the study of colored peoples by whites. The characterization, however, does illustrate the point that the study of kinship systems by anthropologists does not have an obvious value or purpose to those who are studied in this way. In between these two extremes of practical theory and theory without a practical purpose (at least not for those studied) come the range of activities performed in our society by administrators, managers, public service professionals and others whose function mediates between the new knowledge, research, and policies produced by society and the demands generated by the workaday world of government, business, social needs and services.

A final type of legitimation, *symbolic universes,* constitutes the ultimate legitimation of any institutional order. Commonly shared symbolic universes provide explanations which help to integrate otherwise terrifying or unintelligible features of human experience. For individuals, a symbolic universe can serve to integrate death into the reality of one's social existence. This may be done through religion, or through various forms of modern atheism (scientific or political) which allow an individual to account for the death of those close to him as well as to anticipate his own death with a measure of calm and without undue fear. For society as a whole, symbolic universes help to maintain feelings of security and to mitigate situations of potential chaos and terror. When revered leaders die – and especially when they die suddenly or through violence – great care is taken to reaffirm through solemn ceremonies the meaning and continuance of the institutional order itself. In past decades, a number of nations have had to deal with such violent deaths involving political leaders –

John and Robert Kennedy and Martin Luther King in the United States, Anwar el Sadat in Egypt. In Africa and Asia in the 1970s, newly emergent nations witnessed similarly traumatic moments as the founders of the independence movements of the previous decades died or were deposed and suceeded by an altogether different sort of peacetime leader. Symbolic universes are most apparent to us in the special rituals that integrate fearful circumstances into some greater meaningful order.

19.1.2 Alternative Symbolic Universes

"The appearance of an alternative symbolic universe," Berger and Luckmann maintain, "poses a threat because its very existence demonstrates empirically that one's own universe is less than inevitable."[2] An *alternative symbolic universe* arises when a society is confronted in some manner by another society with a distinctively different history. It is not the sort of conflict which occurs within a given society between majority views and those of distinctive and opposed minorities. Differences over opinion and future actions are not the same thing as confrontation with another social order which views one's definitions of reality as absurd or evil or both. More often than not the confrontation with alternative symbolic universes becomes a question of power and, therefore, a question of whose definition can be forced to prevail. This results precisely because there are no higher forms of legitimation to which those in conflict can appeal.

Typically, such confrontations have existed between colonizing states and their colonized clients; and there have been numerous recent occasions where the powerful nations and those emergent nations of the Third World have regarded each other with mutual, though unequal, incomprehension. The United States and Vietnam in past decades, France and Algeria in the 1950s, the Soviet Union and the People's Republic of China since the mid-1960s are examples that come easily to mind. What is important to grasp about these circumstances is that the incomprehension comes about in part because the vast inequalities of strength do not seem to have the expected impact upon the weaker antagonist.

More common than the confrontation of alternative symbolic

universes is the pluralistic structure of most modern societies where *partially different* symbolic universes are maintained in a contentious but mutually accommodating fashion. Mythology, theology, philosophy, and science all represent what Berger and Luckmann call the conceptual machinery of universe-maintenance. It is through such conceptual machinery that differing definitions of reality arise. These symbolic *sub-universes* represent and maintain *sub-societies*; and the *counter-definitions* of reality which arise in a given society from time to time likewise require and promote *counter-societies.* In these cases the mutual accommodation among sub-societies and counter-societies is not a permanent state of affairs, but always a tentative one. Thus, therapy could be included as another form of universe-maintenance, one which concerns itself with identifying individual deviations from "official definitions" of reality and, in varying degrees, tries to adjust these deviations.

At the extremes of universe-maintenance are *nihilation* and *revolution.* Just as therapy attempts to keep everyone inside a given symbolic universe, nihilation attempts to do away with everything outside the same universe. Nihilation proceeds either by denying the "sense" of what goes on outside one's own universe or, more coyly, by attempting to redefine those negations or rejections of one's reality as covert demonstrations of belief or affirmation. Thus, complete rejection of a suitor's attentions may be rationalized by the suitor as only a camouflage for deeper interest. Or, the society that finds itself condemned outright by another society may rationalize this rejection as only a cover for covetousness. By comparison, revolution tends to begin within society as part of a recognized opposition, often through the role of dissident intellectuals and politicians, and frequently ends with these same opposition figures forced to make the change to the role of official legitimators. In this way even in revolutionary change the legitimation process plays a part in the maintenance of symbolic universes and in their transformations as well.

19.2 Community Orders

19.2.1 Epistemic Communities – Holzner

Like types of legitimation, types of social roles provide us with recipes through which to account for our experiences and guide our actions and relations with others. This is no less true for the common man than it is for the scientist. Plumbers and administrators, politicians and philosophers all possess specialized social role models and recipes. The sociologist Burkart Holzner calls our social roles "constructs" which orient our relationships to changing situations and to others.[3]

Holzner believes a social role is defined by two factors, by its *institutional sphere* and by its *particular loyalties.* The business sphere, the political-administrative sphere, the religious sphere, the military sphere, and the educational sphere all define social roles. Institutional spheres provide conventional frames of reference and knowledge. They function much like sub-systems of society, containing their own features of change and stability and working out their own forms of mutual accommodation with other spheres of activity within the same society. In addition, roles are related to loyalties which cut across or transcend those of the specialized institutional spheres. Such loyalties account for our personal commitments and emotional identifications, as well as membership with groups unrelated to situations of work and to the frames of reference of our institutional spheres.

Where the occupants of social roles have both similar frames of reference and similar loyalties, there is an *epistemic community.* Epistemic communities, such as scientific communities, military or medical communities, religious communities, or ideological movements, are characterized by an interlinking of roles, loyalties, and perspectives. In modern industrial societies, most people find themselves belonging to and participating in a variety of epistemic communities to which they are linked by *roles* and also through *channels of communication.*

Channels of communication are crucial to epistemic communities in modern societies because they restrain the flow of information inside and outside a community. All epistemic communities carefully manage the flow of information out of the community. In part this is accomplished through the standardization of the symbolic system; each epistemic community – scientific, religious, or ideological – develops symbolic systems which define and constrain its members' expression and which limit, in turn, the capacity of the surrounding society to fully comperhend its internal activities. What Holzner calls the *reality constructs* of a community are thus the product of its social roles and its modes, codes, and means of communication.

19.2.2 Constructed Communities – Suttles

Communities are defined and constrained not only through their own information networks and shared ideas as Holzner demonstrates, but much more than is commonly acknowledged through the actions and commentary of others external to them. Communities, the sociologist Gerald Suttles says, are *dialogic representations.* Localized communities especially are the result of contradistinctions with other areas and groups; and they are continuously constructed through commentary, including the imputations of adjacent groups, media coverage, spokesmen elected or self-appointed, as well as by other outsiders of consequence – developers, realtors, public officials.[4]

The identity of communities, including the actual naming of neighborhoods, groups or movements, is often the result of outsiders. For differences to be recognized, others must agree. Thus, two factors are powerfully at work in the maintenance of a community order: the role of outsiders and material conditions outside the community in providing a community's self-image; and the role of some formal information channel, such as a community newspaper or group publication that acts as a custodian in promoting a community's sense of integrity, boundaries, and responsibilities – in a term, its reality constructs.

19.2.3 Scientific Communities – Kuhn

Thomas Kuhn's studies of the impact of communication upon the scientific community led him to propose that the scientific community produces its knowledge and its world view simultaneously through what he calls *paradigm creation.*[5] Paradigm is a much debated concept, but like "reality construct" it is intended to point up the way in which the scientific community (despite its romantic claims to truth and pure research) in reality is defined and constrained by the conventions, roles, loyalties, and material circumstances common to most communities. They also differ from conventional communities. Scientific communities are maintained in *paradigm articulation,* through training programs in universities, textbooks, the circulation of work through journals, all of which helps to orient the tasks and perspectives of its members. When questions and challenges arise, *paradigm reconstruction* must take place through the search for new and more adequate explanations for the anomalous evidence (evidence which does not fit with the previously accepted explanations), usually through seeking increasingly narrower conceptual problems and greater detail. Finally, *paradigm transformations, shifts, or revolutions* occur when new insights persuade scientists to create and define new communities (biochemistry or information science, for instance), to produce new texts, training programs, journals, and thus to repeat the process.

It is worth noting that what Kuhn finds distinctive about the scientific community is the importance it gives to argument and dialogue. Although in times of shift from one paradigm to another the situation seems to be characterized not by rational discussion so much as by breakdowns in communication and by the greater importance placed upon persuasion, Kuhn uses precisely this circumstance to distinguish what he calls these *rational forms of persuasion* found in science from the forms of persuasion found elsewhere in society.

19.3 Conclusion

Paradigm, reality construct, and symbolic universe are all examples of the machinery of universe maintenance. They are all modes of communication that stress the reflexiveness of the communication process (the necessary role of self-reference for societies and communities) and underscore the role of feedback (for conservation of meanings, conventions, and practices).

Kuhn's model of the scientific community brings to light the role that communities of experts play in defining and constraining public life. In that such experts counsel government, produce designs, and make judgments on a great many matters affecting others, their influence can have a large impact upon what is thought about, how it is thought about, and upon what is not thought about as well.

Paradigm maintenance is characterized by modes of convergent thinking and paradigm change is identified, at least initially, through modes of divergent thinking making themselves felt. Within the communities concerned with understanding and improving the modes and the means of communication there have been some interesting recent examples of convergent and divergent thinking, the subject of the next chapter.

CHAPTER 20

Research, Designs, and Judgments

20.1 The Paradigm Shift in Communication Research

20.1.1 Roles and Relationships

In recent years it has been suggested that our perspectives on communication may be undergoing something like a paradigm shift.[1] The concept of paradigm is too precise to describe the matters in question, but there does seem to be some genuine shifting of concepts and concerns by a number of researchers and some new and interesting efforts to rethink the basic issues of communication.

The British communications researcher James Halloran insists that all research involves *the right to redefine.*[2] Until recently in the development of communication research, Halloran believes, "doing" has prevailed over "thinking." In part this was the inevitable outcome of the growth of the basic technologies of mass communication worldwide and the subsequent need for research which could provide practical and efficient guidance for administrative and commercial needs. The result, Halloran says, has been a great deal of data collection lacking in both theory and working hypotheses and "usually more concerned with sampling than with conceptualization and with description rather than analysis."[3]

Today by contrast there is a recognized need for more conceptually adequate tools as researchers begin to treat communication processes in a more systematic way and to inquire more deliberately into the various needs for information and sources of information in a society. The mass media constitute one such source, but in order to analyze this rigorously we would have to be able to examine the personal and the social implications of particular political and economic structures in the social system as well as their different institutional organizations. From this viewpoint, media would have to be examined not only as conveyers of information, but as definers of problems, setters of priorities, suggesters of solutions, and general revealers and interpreters of the world at large.

What we need to analyze, Halloran suggests, are both the roles and the relationships involved: on the one hand, the needs defining the role of the communicator at various levels of social life and, on the other hand, the nature and quality of the relationship between the media, its sources, and its audience (including matters of validity, unwitting or inherent bias, accountability, access, and participation). In the past the media have resisted efforts to do such studies. In fact, it is somewhat paradoxical that media professionals, who defend their right to investigate virtually all aspects of society, frequently resist similar scrutiny of their own activities.

Such analyses have become necessary, in part because the various principles that have guided media practices (freedom of the press, free flow of information, and so on) have, like other rights and principles of speech, assembly, and access to information, undergone great changes and continue to do so. Researchers more and more recognize their own role in helping to understand how *principles,* such as the various freedoms of communication and information, are related to *actual practices* at a given time in society. Halloran has suggested, for instance, that we ought to be examining all these sectors of society which provide us with symbolic representations in light of these principles. In short, this is an argument that researchers must begin to pay attention to the *consequences* of our communication practices.

20.1.2 Understanding Social Change – Briggs

The impact of the means of communication on social change, Lord Briggs has said, can be understood only in terms of the varied ways in which individuals and communities select from it, perceive it, and use it.[4] The problem this raises is how to move from the broad generalizations which have dominated the sorts of macro-research done in the past to what he calls a detailed and comparative study of particular structures and particular places. To this end, he believes that research on social change provides us with four comprehensive approaches:

(1) marxist approaches, emphasizing the relationship of economic and non-economic forces and oriented toward *action*, in this case, toward devising strategies for social change;
(2) evolutionist approaches, characterized by the assumption that all countries eventually pass through *stages* of development (such as those of the developed countries), but containing no explicit link between theory and action, although such theories have been used in relation to the diffusion of technologies and consumer goods;
(3) systems approaches generally involving the attempt to analyze a number of relevant variables and to relate them in the form of a *model*, which can be used for making recommendations to communication practitioners and for designs; and
(4) comparative historical approaches through historically and geographically specific *case studies* from a number of theoretical points of view, critically compared.

Briggs believes that the concerns with social change have now convincingly shifted in the direction of the latter approach. Harsher realities have replaced the optimism about social goals in much of the decolonized world. It is now recognized that there are many different strategies to development and, consequently, there is today greater emphasis on *alternative strategies* within a particular country. Additionally, there is a stronger concern for what a Director-General of UNESCO, Amadow M'Bow, has called *endogenous creativity* – the recognition of the potentials *within a culture*, so that future development will not jeopardize present identity.

It is more apparent today that social change and development cannot rely upon the theories developed in the Western world. The concepts of information and education embedded in these theories are culturally specific and too general to grasp the differences within the range of other cultures and societies – hence, the need for comparative analyses. At the same time, our efforts to understand the role of media in social change in the developing world needs to be placed within the historical trends of the past hundred years, which have seen the flow of cultural-informational materials on a largely one-way course – thus, the need for historical perspective.

20.1.3 The Policymaking Dilemma – Cater

More and more we must recognize, Douglass Cater says, that the important policy issues are emerging from disputes over what he calls the *organizing principles* of our media.[5] Moreover, the difficulties we experience in finding resolutions to these disputes, as for instance when they occur between nations, is compounded by the pace of development of new technologies, including the more commonly known cases of direct broadcast satellites and cable systems. Technologies such as these set contrary forces into motion. On the one side they generate a centralizing force, potentially placing greater power in the control of political or corporate elites. On the other side, they generate a decentralizing force, on the grounds that providing people with more information more quickly ought to make them eligible to participate more fully in the decision-making process. In fact, the interactive or two-way design features of both the newer satellite and cable technologies make this latter argument even more compelling.

Cater believes the central difficulty for policy and policymakers faced with these sorts of issues and potentials is how to provide *adequate organizing principles* for our media systems without becoming bound up in forms of organization which invalidate the principles in practice. As a former editor and journalist, Cater points to the example of the First Amendment of the United States Constitution which forbids the Congress to make laws abridging freedom of the press and of speech. A contradiction, he argues, has arisen in the first amendment because public policy toward freedom of the press has allowed for increasing monopolizing of ownership, with the consequence that in many North American communities there is now a total monopoly of newspaper ownership. Since the press is an important local means of free speech in modern society, the effectiveness of "free speech" may well be diminished by the noncompetitiveness of the "free press." What Cater wishes to draw attention to is the interrelatedness of our communication practices and our organizing principles. To see that these matters do not stand in isolation from each other, he believes, is the first step toward more adequate conceptions of communication policy. Not to conscientiously make policy in this way in an age of increasing interdependency, Cater warns, simply allows policy to be made by inadvertence – or by special interests.

20.2 Designs and Judgments

20.2.1 A Note on Intervention

Communication research is not a neutral activity. It constantly produces designs and judgments. These designs and judgments range from technical problems to legal-political and cultural matters, from questions of appropriate technology to the right to communicate and the right to information, all matters related to the interfacing of communication processes within society. Two issues in particular have surfaced in recent years as the communication infrastructure of technology and institutions has begun to approximate a world system – gatekeeping issues and periphery issues.

20.2.2 Gatekeeping Issues

"Freedom of information," the UNESCO declaration on news organizations affirmed in November of 1978, "is a fundamental human right and is the touchstone of all the freedoms to which the United Nations is consecrated; freedom of information requires as an indispensable element the willingness and capacity to employ its privileges without abuse." But, as South American media researcher Luis Beltrán has pointed out there is much more agreement about the meaning of information than about the meaning of freedom in such policy statements.[6] Part of the dispute over the meaning of freedom results from what is sometimes referred to as the *gatekeeper question*: who has access to send the information and who has access to receive it? In principle, it is believed that the more options individuals have at their disposal as senders and receivers, the greater the degree of freedom they can be said to have. Contrarily, the fewer the options as senders or receivers or both, the lower the degree of communicational freedom. Beltrán suggests that there are three main factors by which the sending and receiving options in a society – and thus the function of gatekeeping – can be assessed: (1) interference, (2) ownership distribution, and (3) the existence of sources.

Interference refers to the restriction or elimination of communication options. Since all information, as previous chapters have documented, is the result of selection, interpretation, and construction, the notion of interference involves the active suppression of materials through direct or indirect forms of censorship. *Ownership distribution,* on the other hand, indicates the extent to which the sending options are widely held in a society, or narrowly held through direct government control or through accumulation within centralized corporate structures. In Latin America, as in the United States, ownership of basic media is almost exclusively private, by contrast with the mixed systems of public and private ownership in Canada, Australia, and much of Europe, and with the state-controlled or monitored systems in most of Asia, and with those special systems, largely intended for educational and community uses, in parts of Africa and South America. Finally, *the existence of sources* indicates the availability of information resources that can be drawn upon for sending and for receiving purposes. Here, information resources may vary between regions of a country (urban and rural, for instance), between groupings in the population (the aged and other minorities), and between classes. A restriction on senders is also a restriction on receivers, and vice versa. This is why the *relative freedom* Beltrán is attempting to identify must be seen as a function of the interrelationship of senders, receivers, and sources in a given society.

20.2.3 Periphery Issues

As important as the freedom of information issues are those issues associated with *the flow of communication.* In fact, it has been the global anomaly of a predominantly one-way flow of media materials from northern countries to southern ones that provoked the previously mentioned UNESCO declaration to call "for the establishment of a new and greater reciprocity in the flow of information . . . to correct the inequalities in the flow of information to and from developing countries and between those countries."[7] The debate over "free" versus "balanced" flow is more than a disagreement over principles. "Balanced" can mean little more than what the state censor or propagandist dictates and "free" may obscure the ways in which those who control large media operations constantly restrain the development of technologies providing greater access or decentralization of control. At issue is not simply a matter of flows between Northern Hemispheric centers and Southern Hemispheric peripheries, but among peripheries themselves and among centers and peripheries within countries.

Perhaps the major point made by people on the peripheries is what might be called a distinction between the *right to communication* and the *right to communicate.* The right to communication, to have access to sources of information, has been a strong demand made by marginal areas. If communication is a right, it is a right for all. Thus, it is argued that those in inaccessible areas have a right to the resources of communication that others enjoy. The right to communication has also become identified with the right of access to specialized information. Rural communities have demanded access to the information resources of the city for local health and legal needs as well as for entertainment; and in the United States the passage of "right to know" legislation has given private citizens access to government information on themselves.

The right to communicate, by comparison, has had its origins on the peripheries, but in a different way. Both developing countries and regional minorities within developed countries have, in recent years, argued for their right to utilize communication resources in more autonomous ways. Peripheral areas or peripheral groups (peripheral to the centers and to the majorities, that is) have maintained that the means of communication ought to facilitate communication among themselves as well as with the centers. Otherwise, it is argued, national communication systems will remain unbalanced in favor of center-margin relations, thus failing to respect and encourage the needs and character of indigenous cultures. The Inuit and Indian peoples in Canada's northern areas, for instance, have used the design potentials of satellite technology to argue that the interactive media links they make possible should be used to encourage two-way communication among the Arctic areas and northern peoples and not to perpetuate historical patterns of North-South, or periphery-center relations.

20.3 Conclusion

If, as it has been argued by some of the researchers and practitioners in this text, the means of communication serve to reduce uncertainty in matters requiring judgment or choice, many of the issues of rights and principles – such as those raised by developing countries through the United Nations or those raised by minorities at home – concern the question of how best to deploy the limited potentials we now see in these means of communication for reasonable as well as practical ends. In part these are all instances of rethinking the relation of principles and practices.

CHAPTER 21

The Human Conversation

21.1 A Final Note on Research

Much of the material in this book has been intended to underscore the sorts of conceptual resources that in recent times have come to bear upon the issues of communication. At the same time, it has been argued that the intellectual task of gaining access to the conceptual world of others and the more practical task of conversing with them, should be accepted as interdependent ones. The intellectual task may place greater emphasis upon understanding meaning and the practical task may see its broader purpose in the actual improvement of communication; yet, there is a sense today that we are not dealing with an equation of *either* intellectual *or* practical tasks, but rather an equation of *both* intellectual *and* practical tasks. If the reader has gotten this far, perhaps two further examples will be permitted in place of reaching for conclusions, examples both pertinent and self-critical.

21.2 Mutual Adjustments

Several years ago an American political scientist, Charles Lindblom, wrote an eloquent book entitled *The Intelligence of Democracy* in which he gently warned his fellow professionals about a blind spot in their thinking if they went on focusing their analyses, designs, and judgments regarding the social world exclusively upon those centrally coordinated mechanisms and institutions (such as communication networks, information flows, and audience effects) through which modern societies attempted to manage aspects of their interaction. Lindblom felt strongly that this bias toward seeing human activity solely in terms of the central forms of coordination through which people are governed, regulated and otherwise influenced and controlled could blind us to the many natural tendencies in society toward coordination, consensus, and commitment. "People," he said, "can coordinate with each other without anyone's coordinating them, without a dominant common purpose, and without rules that fully prescribe their relations to each other."[1] Lindblom called this a natural tendency toward *mutual adjustment.*

Until recently most researchers, designers, and policy-makers concerned with the practical issues of communication have found themselves concentrating upon the mechanisms of central coordination; consequently, most of our designs and judgments have been prepared and proposed within the context of the policies and practices of those centrally coordinated institutions. Much communication technology developed in this century has been adopted and adapted to improve upon these basic strategies of coordination. This preoccupation with management and the material basis for it, when it becomes a totalizing vision of communication, leads us to forget that centrally coordinated media and other such information systems are only one aspect of the total communication happening in society. By mistaking the part these systems play for the whole of the process or in taking centrally coordinated messages and meanings as the only ones that matter, we too frequently have overlooked the natural capacity in society for mutual adjustment. Defining centrally coordinated communication as the predominant interactional environment has led us as researchers and practitioners into a century-long preoccupation with manipulative communication strategies, particularly evident in the rise of centrally coordinated forms of publicity and persuasion; and evident as well in our preoccupations with the effects and consequences that such manipulative communication strategies seem to have for us as societies and individuals.

All of this is, of course, important. Yet, much of what constitutes the everyday life of society goes on without and even in spite of these communication strategies or any other form of central coordination. Even in international trade most matters are still worked out among the trading partners themselves. In courts of law, the thousands of judges who render all manner of rulings on a daily basis proceed largely by keeping an eye on one another, adjusting to one another's interpretations, and only occasionally by referring to the decisions of higher courts. Laws exist, but their interpretation (at least under conditions reasonably free from coercion) is largely a matter of mutual adjustment within the judicial community itself. The disputes and conciliations of everyday work and leisure are replete with similar examples. As this text has tried to argue, when and wherever people constitute themselves in interaction with others, the occasion is always potentially one for mutual adjustment through communication. As much as the liar or the cheat depends upon the orientation of others toward honesty and truth, the very possibility of manipulation through communication depends upon a more basic human tendency toward mutual adjustment.

21.3 Flows

The concept of mutual adjustment emphasizes the way in which consensus and commitment are as much the outcome of everyday human interaction as they are the result of centrally coordinated communication strategies. At the same time we should not underestimate the part played by the formal networks of information and communication in the formation of consensus and commitment. Today these networks and the flows they make possible interpenetrate a global variety of community and institutional orders characterized by widely divergent ways of life. As a result, there are many misunderstandings.

It would be regrettable, however, if these flows should break down. Flows are often spoken of as if they were only information content, commodities, manipulation, and influence. They are much more than that. Flows help *maintain our own traditions*, some part of which depends upon the technical means and technical skills we have available to us. Flows also *mediate betweem different traditions,* a large part of which depends today upon the technological and organizational infrastructure of communication and our agreements for its use. When flows break down or cease altogether, the result is that our *intersubjective understanding* either collapses or hardens into fixed and frozen positions.[2] Maintaining and extending intersubjective understanding within and among the human community is, thus, partly a matter of the flows themselves.

It seems reasonable to expect that our concerns *for* communication can serve these intersubjective ends if we can manage to remember that the search for concepts and the search for structures are *not* separate tasks.

Bibliography

Adorno, Theodor W. "The Stars Down to Earth: The *Los Angeles Times* Astrology Column." *Telos,* 19 (1974), pp. 13-90.

Allport, G.W., and T.F. Pettigrew. "Cultural Influence on the Perception of Movement: the Trapezoidal Illusion among Zulus." *Journal of Abnormal and Social Psychology,* 55 (1957), pp. 104-13.

Ames, Jr., Adelbert. "Visual Perception and the Rotating Trapezoidal Window." *Psychology Monographs,* 65 (1951), pp. 1-31.

Appleman, P., ed. *Darwin, a Norton Critical Edition.* New York: Norton, 1970.

Asch, Solomon. "Effects of Group Pressure upon the Modification and Distortion of Judgments." In *Dimensions in Communication: Readings.* Ed. J.H. Campbell and H. W. Hepler. Belmont, CA: Wadsworth, 1970.

Barnlund, Dean C. "A transactional Model of Communication." In *Foundations of Communication Theory.* Ed. K. Sereno and C. Mortensen. New York: Harper and Row, 1970, pp. 83-102.

Barthes, Roland. *Elements of Semiology.* London: Cape, 1967.

———. *Systême de la mode.* Paris: Editions due Seuil, 1967.

Bateson, Gregory. *Mind and Nature.* New York: Dutton, 1979.

———. *Steps to an Ecology of Mind.* New York: Ballantine, 1972.

Beltrán, Louis. "Communication Research in Latin America: The Blindfolded Inquiry?" In *Internationale Wissenschaftliche Konferenz,* der Anteil der Massenmedien bei der Herausbildung des Bewusstseins in der sich wandelnden welt. Leipzig: Karl-Marx Universität, 1974, pp. 370-93.

Benge, Roland C. *Communication and Identity.* London: Bingley, 1972.

Berelson, Bernard, and others. *Voting.* Chicago: University of Chicago Press, 1954.

Berger, John, and others. *Ways of Seeing.* London: BBC and Penguin, 1972.

Berger, Peter L., and Thomas Luckmann. *The Social Construction of Reality.* Garden City, NY: Anchor Books, 1966.

Bernstein, Basel. "Elaborated and Restricted Codes: Their Social Origins and Some Consequences." In *Communication and Culture.* Ed. A.G. Smith. New York: Holt, Rinehart, and Winston, 1966.

Birdwhistell, Ray L. *Kinesics and Context.* Philadelphia: University of Pennsylvania Press, 1970.

———. "Some Body Motion Elements Accompanying Spoken American English." In *Communication: Concepts and Perspectives.* Ed. L. Thayer. Wash.: Spartan Books, 1967.

Böll, Heinrich. *The Lost Honor of Katerina Blum.* New York: McGraw-Hill, 1975.

Boorstin, Daniel J. *The Image – A Guide to Pseudo-Events in America.* New York: Atheneum, 1971.

Bramsted, E.K. *Goebbels and National Socialist Propaganda: 1925-45.* East Lansing, Michigan: Michigan State University Press, 1965.

Briggs, Lord Asa. "Broadcasting and Social Change: Relationships under Review." In *Symposium on the Cultural Role of Broadcasting, Summary Report.* Tokyo: Hoso-Bunka Foundation, 1978, pp. 70-78.

Brouwer, Martin. "Prolegomena to a Theory of Mass Communication." In *Communication: Concepts and Perspectives.* Ed. Lee Thayer. Washington: Spartan Books, 1967, pp. 227-40.

Budd, Richard, and Brent Ruben, ed. *Approaches to Human Communication.* New York: Spartan Books, 1972.

Burke, Kenneth. "Dramatism." In *Communication: Concepts and Perspectives.* Ed. Lee Thayer. Washington: Spartan Books, 1967.

Campbell, James H. and H.W. Hepler, ed. *Dimensions in Communication: Readings.* Belmont, CA: Wadsworth, 1970.

Carey, James W. "Canadian Communication Theory: Extensions and Interpretations of Harold Innis." In *Studies in Canadian Communication.* Ed. G.J. Robinson and D.F. Theall. Montréal: McGill Programme in Communication, 1975, pp. 27-59.

———. "Communication and Culture." *Communication Research,* Vol. 2, No. 2 (1975), 1973-91.

———. "Culture, Geography, and Communications: The Work of Harold Innis in an American Context." In *Culture, Communication, and Dependency – The Tradition of H.A. Innis.* Ed. W. Melody, and others. Norwood, N.J.: Ablex 1981.

Cater, Douglass. "The Future of Communications Policy." In *Symposium on the Cultural Role of Broadcasting, Summary Report.* Tokyo: Hoso-Bunka Foundation, 1978, pp. 124-30.

Crowley, D.J. "The Communication of Bias and the Bias of Communication." In *Communication Studies in Canada/Recherche en Communication au Canada.* Ed. L. Salter. Toronto: Butterworths, 1981.

———. "Harold Innis in the Modern Communications Perspective." In *Culture, Communication, and Dependency.*

———. "Mass Communication and Domination." *Communication Research* Vol. 7, No. 2 (1980).

———. *Communication Theory III: Semiology.* Montréal: Centre for Learning and Development, 1975.

Dallmayr, Fred, and Thomas McCarthy. ed. *Understanding and Social Inquiry.*

Notre Dame: Notre Dame University Press, 1977.

Dance, Frank, ed. *Human Communication Theory: Original Essays.* New York: Holt, Rinehart and Winston, 1967.

Dance, Frank, and C.E. Larson, ed. *The Functions of Human Communication* New York: Holt, Rinehart and Winston, 1976.

Deutsch, Karl. *The Nerves of Government.* New York: The Free Press, 1966.

Dewey, John. *The Public and Its Problems.* Chicago: Swallow Press, 1927.

Duncan, Hugh D. "Communication and Social Order." In *The Human Dialogue.* Ed. F.W. Matson and A. Montagu. New York: The Free Press, 1967.

Eco, Umberto. "Can Television Teach?" Schools Television Conference. London: June, 1978. Unpublished transcript.

Fearing, Frank. "Towards a Psychological Theory of Human Communication." In *Interpersonal Communication: Survey and Studies.* Ed. Dean C. Barnlund. Boston: Houghton Mifflin, 1968.

Felstehausen, Herman. "Conceptual Limits of Development Communications Theory." *Sociologia Ruralis,* Vol. 3, No. 1 (1973), 39-53.

Festinger, Leon. "Cognitive Dissonance." *Scientific American,* 160 (1962), pp. 93-102.

Friedenberg, Edgar J. *Deference to Authority.* White Plains, NY: Sharpe, 1980.

Friendly, Fred W. *Due to Circumstances Beyond Our Control.* New York: Vintage, 1967.

Furth, Hans. *Thinking Without Language.* New York: the Free Press, 1966.

Geertz, Clifford. *The Interpretation of Cultures.* New York: Basic Books, 1973.

Giglioli, P.P., ed. *Language and Social Context.* Baltimore: Penguin, 1972.

Glascow University Media Group. *Bad News.* London: Routledge and Kegan Paul, 1980.

Goffman, Erving. *Asylums.* Garden City, NY: Anchor, 1961.

Gogel, W.C. "The Adjacency Principle in Visual Perception." *Scientific American,* 238 (1978), pp. 126-37.

Gombrich, E.H. *Art and Illusion; A Study in the Psychology of Pictorial Representation.* New York: Pantheon Books, 1969.

———. "The Visual Image." *Scientific American,* September (1972), pp. 82-96.

Goody, Jack. *The Domestication of the Savage Mind.* Cambridge: Cambridge University Press, 1978.

Gouldner, Alvin. *The Dialectics of Ideology and Technology.* New York: Seabury, 1976.

Greenberg, J.H., ed. *Universals of Language.* Cambridge, MA: MIT Press, 1963.

Gubach, Thomas H. *The International Film Industry: Western Europe and America since 1945.* Bloomington, IN: Indiana University Press, 1969.

Habermas, Jürgen. *Legitimation Crisis.* Boston: Beacon Press, 1979.

———. "Vorbereitende Bemerrkungen zu einer Theorie der kommunikativen Kompetenz." In *Theorie der Gesselschaft oder Sozialtechnologie.* Jürgen Habermas and Nikolas Luhmann. Frankfurt: Suhrkamp, 1971.

Hall, Edward. "Silent Assumptions in Social Communication." In *The Human Dialogue*. Ed. F.W. Matson and A. Montagu. New York: The Free Press, 1967, pp. 491-505.

————. *The Silent Language*. New York: Doubleday, 1959.

Halloran, James D. *Mass Media and Society*. Leicester: Leicester University Press, 1974.

Heyer, Paul. "Innis and the History of Communication: Antecedents, Parallels, and Unsuspected Biases." In *Cutture, Communication, and Dependency*.

Holzner, Burkart. *Reality Construction in Society*. Cambridge, MA: Schenkman, 1972.

Horkheimer, Max, and Theodor Adorno. *Dialectic of Enlightenment*. New York: Herder and Herder, 1972.

Hovland, Carl. and others. *Communication and Persuasion*. New Haven: Yale University Press, 1953.

Hymes, Dell. *Foundations in Sociolinguistics: An Ethnographic Approach*. Philadelphia: University of Pennsylvania Press, 1974.

————. "On the Origins and Foundations of Inequality Among Speakers." *Daedalus*, Vol. 102, No.3 (1973), 59-86.

Innis, Harold A. *The Bias of Communication*. Toronto: University of Toronto Press, 1951.

————. *Empire and Communication*. Oxford: Calrendon, 1950.

Jakobson, Roman. 'Verbal Communication." *Scientific American*, September (1972), pp. 73-80.

Katz, Elihu, and Paul Lazarsfeld. *Personal Influence*. Glencoe, IL: The Free Press, 1955.

Keller, Helen. *The Story of My Life*. New York: Doubleday, 1954.

Klapper, J.T. *The Effects of Mass Communication*. New York: The Free Press, 1960.

Klapp, Orin. *Opening and Closing*. New York: Oxford University Press, 1978.

Kuhn, Thomas. *The Structure of Scientific Revolutions*. Chicago: University of Chicago Press, 1970.

Kuhns, William. *The Post-Industrial Prophets: Interpretation of Technology*. New York: Weybright and Talley, 1971.

Kunreuther, Howard. "Changing Societal Consequences of Risks from Natural Hazards." *American Academy of Political and Social Science Annals*, 443 (1979), pp. 104-16.

————. "Limited Knowledge and Insurance Protection." *Public Policy*, 24 (1976), pp. 227-61.

Langer, Susanne. *Philosophy in a New Key*. Cambridge, MA: Harvard University Press, 1942.

Lasswell, Harold D. *Politics: who gets what, when, how*. New York: McGraw-Hill, 1936.

Lazarsfeld, Paul, and others. *The People's Choice*. New York: Columbia University Press, 1948.

Leach, Edmund. *Culture and Communication*. Cambridge: Cambridge University Press, 1976.

Lerner, Daniel. *The Passing of Traditional Society*. New York: The Free Press, 1964.

Lewin, Kurt. "Channels of Group Life." *Human Relations*, Vol. 1, No. 2 (1947).

Lindblom, Charles. *The Intelligence of Democracy*. New York: The Free Press, 1965.

Lowenthal, Leo. *Literature, Popular Culture and Society*. New York: Prentice Hall, 1961.

MacBride Commission (International Commission for the Study of Communication Problems). *Many Voices, One World*. London: Kogan Page, 1980.

McLean, Malcolm. and H. Toch. "Perception, Communication, and Educational Research: A Transactional View." In *Dimensions in Communication*. Ed. J.H. Campbell, and H.W. Hepler. Belmont, CA: Wadsworth, 1970.

March, James, and Herbert Simon. *Organizations*. New York: Wiley, 1958.

Matson, F. W. and A. Montagu. *The Human Dialogue*, New York: The Free Press, 1967.

Mattelart, Armand, and S. Siegelaub, ed. *Communication and Class Struggle*. New York: International General, 1979.

McAnany, Emile, ed. *Communications in the Rural Third World*. New York: Praeger, 1980.

McClelland, David. *The Achieving Society*. New York: Van Nostrand, 1961.

McLuhan, Marshall, *Understanding Media: the Extensions of Man*. New York: Signet, 1964.

Mead, George Herbert. "Thought, Communication and the Significant Symbol." In *The Human Dialogue*. New York: The Free Press, 1967, pp. 397-403.

Melody, William, and others. *Culture, Communication and Dependency: The Tradition of H.A. Innis*. Norwood, NJ: Ablex, 1981.

Miller, George. *The Psychology of Communication: Seven Essays*. New York: Basic Books, 1967.

Morris, Charles. *Signs, Language and Behavior*. New York: Prentice-Hall, 1946.

Mueller, Claus. *The Politics of Communication*. New York: Oxford, 1973.

O'Hara, John. *Appointment in Samarra*. New York: Gosset and Dunlap, 1934.

Park, Robert E. *Society: Collective Behavior, News and Opinion, Sociology and Modern Society*. Glencoe, IL: The Free Press, 1955.

Percy, Walker. *The Message in the Bottle – How Queer Man Is, How Queer Language Is, and What One Has To Do With the Other*. New York: Farrar, Straus and Giroux, 1975.

Piaget, Jean. *Psychology and Epistemology*. New York: Grossman, 1971.

Rapoport, Anatol, and others. *Prisoner's Dilemma: A Study in Conflict and Cooperation*. Ann Arbor: University of Michigan Press, 1965.

Rogers, Everett, and L. Kincaid. *Communication Networks*. New York: The Free Press, 1981.

Ruben, Brent. "General Systems Theory." In *Approaches to Human Communication*. Ed. Richard Budd and Brent Ruben. New York: Spartan Books, 1972.

Ruesch, Jurgen. and Gregory Bateson. *Communication: The Social Matrix*

of Psychiatry. New York: Norton, 1951.
Sahlins, Marshall D. *Culture and Practical Reason*. Chicago: University of Chicago Press, 1976.
Saussure, Ferdinand de. *Course in General Linguistics*. New York: McGraw-Hill, 1966.
Schiller, Herbert. *Communication and Cultural Domination*. White Plains, NY: International Arts and Science Press, 1976.
Schramm, Wilbur. *The Process and Effects of Mass Communication*. Urbana, IL: University of Illinois Press, 1954.
Schutz, Alfred. *Collected Papers, Volume I: The Problem of Social Reality*. The Hague: Nijhoff, 1962.
Schwartz, Tony. *The Responsive Cord*. Garden City, NY: Anchor Books, 1973.
Searle, John. "What is a Speech Act?" In *Language and Social Context*. Ed. P.P. Giglioli. Baltimore: Penguin, 1972, pp. 136-54.
Sennett, Richard. *The Fall of Public Man*. New York: Knopf, 1974.
Sereno, K., and C. Mortensen, ed. *Foundations of Communication Theory* New York: Harper and Row, 1970.
Shands, Hanley. "Outline of a General Theory of Human Communication: Implications of Normal and Pathological Schizogenesis." In *Communication: Concepts and Perspectives*. Ed. Lee Thayer. Washington: Spartan Books, 1967.
Shannon, Claude, and Warren Weaver. *The Mathematical Theory of Communication*. Urbana, IL: University of Illinois Press, 1949.
Simon, Herbert A. *Administrative Behavior*. New York: Macmillan, 1959.
———. *The Sciences of the Artificial*. Cambridge, MA: MIT Press, 1969.
Smith, Alfred G. *Communication and Culture*. New York: Holt, Rinehart and Winston, 1966.
Smith, R. "Mythic Elements in TV News." *Journal of Communication*, Vol. 29, No. 1 (1979), 75-82.
Suttles, Gerald. *The Social Construction of Communities*. Chicago: University of Chicago Press, 1972.
Terrace, Herbert. *Nim: A Chimpanzee Who Learned Sign Language*. New York: Knopf, 1980.
Thayer, Lee, ed. *Communication: Concepts and Perspectives*. Washington: Spartan Books, 1967.
Theall, Donald F. *The Medium is the Rear-View Mirror*. Montréal: McGill-Queens Press, 1971.
Tinbergen, E. A. and N. Tinbergen. *Early Childhood Autism: An Ethological Approach*. Berlin: Paul Parey, 1972.
Tuchman, Gaye. *Making News*. New York: The Free Press, 1978.
Tunstall, Jeremy. *The Media are American: Anglo-American Media in the World*. London: Constable, 1977.
Tversky, Amos, and Daniel Kahneman. "Judgment under Uncertainty: Heuristics and Bias." *Science*, 185 (1974), pp. 1124-1131.
Tylor, Edward. *Researches into the Early History of Mankind and the Development of Civilization*. Chicago: University of Chicago Press, 1964.
Von Senden, Marius. *Space and Sight*. London: Methuen, 1960.

Vygotsky, Lev S. *Mind in Society: The Development of Higher Psychological Processes.* Cambridge, MA: Harvard University Press, 1978.

Watzlawick, Paul, *How Real Is Real?* New York: Vintage, 1976.

————, and others. *Change: Principles of Problem Formation and Problem Solution.* New York: Norton, 1974.

————, and others. *Pragmatics of Human Communication.* New York: Norton, 1967.

White, David Manning. "The 'Gate Keeper': A Case Study in the Selection of News." *Journalism Quarterly*, 41 (1950), pp. 325-35.

Whorf, Benjamin Lee. "The Name of the Situation as Affecting Behavior." In *Social Psychology through Symbolic Interaction.* Ed. G. Stone and H. Farbermann. Toronto: Xerox College Publishing, 1970.

Wiener, Norbert. "Cybernetics and Society." In *The Human Dialogue.* Ed. F.W. Matson and A. Montagu. New York: The Free Press, 1967.

————. *The Human Use of Human Beings.* Boston: Houghton Mifflin, 1950.

Williams, Raymond. *Communications,* Baltimore: Penguin, 1962.

————. *The Country and the City.* New York: Oxford, 1973.

————. *Marxism and Literature.* Oxford: Oxford University Press, 1977.

————. *Television: Technology and Cultural Form.* London: Fontana, 1974.

Notes

INTRODUCTION

1. L. Thayer, "Communication and Organization Theory," in *Human Communication Theory: Original Essays*, ed. F.E.X. Dance (NY: Holt, Rinehart and Winston, 1967), p.83.

CHAPTER 1

1. P. Appleman (ed.), *Darwin, a Norton Critical Edition* (NY: Norton, 1970). So complete has been our recent conversion to Darwin's metaphor that it is sometimes difficult to bear in mind that we in the so-called Western World are the only peoples who believe that we are indeed risen from monkeys and savages. The others, the anthropologist Marshall Sahlins reminds us, continue to believe they are descended from gods and angels. M.D. Sahlins, *Culture and Practical Reason* (Chicago: Univ. of Chicago, 1976).
2. N. Wiener, *The Human Use of Human Beings* (Boston: Houghton Mifflin, 1950), pp. 15-27.
3. N. Wiener, "Cybernetics and Society," in *The Human Dialogue*, ed. F.W. Matson and A. Montagu (NY: The Free Press, 1967), pp. 15-23.
4. K. Deutsch, *The Nerves of Government* (NY: The Free Press, 1966), ch. 5.
5. A. Ames, Jr., "Visual Perception and the Rotating Trapezoidal Window," *Psychology Monographs*, 65 (1951), 1-31.
6. G.W. Allport and T.F. Pettigrew, "Cultural Influence on the Perception of Movement: the Trapezoidal Illusion among Zulus," *Journal of Abnormal and Social Psychology*, 55 (1957), 104-13.

7. H. Toch and M.S. MacLean, "Perception, Communication, and Educational Research: A Transactional View," in *Dimensions in Communication*, ed. J.H. Campbell and H.W. Hepler (Belmont: Wadsworth 1970).
8. Deutsch, ch. 11.
9. B. Ruben, "General Systems Theory," in *Approaches to Human Communication*, ed. R. Budd and B. Ruben (NY: Spartan Books, 1972), pp. 130-34.

CHAPTER 2

1. A. Schutz, *Collected Papers, Volume I: The Problem of Social Reality* (The Hague: Nijhoff, 1962).
2. S. Asch, "Effects of Group Pressure upon the Modification and Distortion of Judgments," in *Dimensions in Communication: Readings*, ed. J.H. Campbell and H.W. Hepler (Belmont, CA: Wadsworth, 1970).
3. L. Festinger, "Cognitive Dissonance," *Scientific American*, 160 (1962).
4. F. Fearing, "Towards a Psychological Theory of Human Communication," in *Interpersonal Communication: Survey and Studies*, ed. D.C. Barnlund (Boston: Houghton Mifflin, 1968), pp. 30-44.
5. A. Rapoport and others, *Prisoner's Dilemma: A Study in Conflict and Cooperation* (Ann Arbor: University of Michigan Press, 1965).
6. K. Lewin, *Experiments on Autocratic and Democratic Atmospheres* (Columbus: Merrill, 1938); Lewis, *Resolving Social Conflicts: Selected Papers on Group Dynamics* (London: Souvenir Press, 1973).
7. E.J. Friedenberg, *Deference to Authority* (White Plains: Sharpe, 1980), ch. 3.
8. H. Kunreuther, "Limited Knowledge and Insurance Protection," *Public Policy*, 24 (1976), pp. 227-61; Kunreuther, "Changing Societal Consequences of Risks from Natural Hazards," *American Academy of Political and Social Science Annals*, 443 (1979), pp. 104-16.
9. H.A. Simon, *Administrative Behavior* (NY: Macmillan, 1959).

CHAPTER 3

1. H. Shands, "Outline of a General Theory of Human Communication: Implications of Normal and Pathological Schizogenesis," in *Communication: Concepts and Perspectives*, ed. L. Thayer (Washington: Spartan Books, 1967), pp. 97-134.
2. G.H. Mead, "Thought, Communication and the Significant Symbol," in *The Human Dialogue*, ed. F.W. Matson (NY: The Free Press, 1967), pp. 397-403.
3. M. von Senden, *Space and Sight* (London: Methuen, 1960).
4. F.E.X. Dance and C.E. Larson, *The Functions of Human Communication* (NY: Holt, Rinehart and Winston, 1976), ch. 4.
5. Shands, pp. 97-134.

6. E. Goffman, *The Presentation of Self in Everyday Life* (Garden City, NY: Doubleday, 1959), pp. 1-16.
7. J. Habermas, *Legitimation Crisis* (Boston: Beacon Press, 1979), ch. 1.

CHAPTER 4

1. E. Tylor, *Researches into the Early History of Mankind and the Development of Civilization* (Chicago: University of Chicago Press, 1964).
2. J. Goody, *The Domestication of the Savage Mind* (Cambridge: Cambridge University Press, 1978), pp. 1-18.
3. C. Morris, *Signs, Language and Behavior* (NY: Prentice-Hall, 1946), pp. 18-25.
4. D.J. Crowley, *Semiotics* (Montreal: McGill Center for Learning and Development, 1975).
5. S. Langer, *Philosophy in a New Key* (Cambridge: Harvard University Press, 1942), chs. 2 and 3.

CHAPTER 5

1. H.D. Lasswell, *Politics; Who Gets What, When, How* (NY: McGraw-Hill, 1936).
2. K. Lewin, "Channels of Group Life," *Human Relations,* Vol. 1, No. 2 (1947).
3. D.M. White, "The 'Gate Keeper': A Case Study in the Selection of News," *Journalism Quarterly,* 41 (1950), pp. 325-35.
4. P. Lazarsfeld, B. Berelson, and H. Gaudet, *The People's Choice* (NY: Columbia University Press, 1948); B. Berelson, P. Lazarsfeld, and W.N. McPhee, *Voting* (Chicago: University of Chicago Press, 1954).
5. C. Hovland, I.L. Janis, and H.H. Kelley, *Communication and Persuasion* (New Haven: Yale University Press, 1953), ch. 8.
6. E. Katz and P. Lazarsfeld, *Personal Influence* (Glencoe: The Free Press, 1955).
7. J.T. Klapper, *The Effects of Mass Communication* (NY: The Free Press, 1960).
8. M. Brouwer, "Prolegomena to a Theory of Mass Communication," in *Communication: Concepts and Perspectives,* ed. L. Thayer (Wash.: Spartan Books, 1967), pp. 227-40.
9. B. Westley and M. MacLean, "A Conceptual Model for Communication Research," *Journalism Quarterly,* 34 (1957), pp. 31-38.
10. E.K. Bramsted, *Goebbels and National Socialist Propaganda: 1925-1945,* (East Lansing: Michigan State University Press, 1965).

CHAPTER 6

1. C. Shannon and W. Weaver, *The Mathematical Theory of Communication* (Urbana: University of Illinois Press, 1949); N. Wiener, *Cybernetics* (Cambridge: M.I.T. Press, 1948).
2. W. Schramm, *The Process and Effects of Mass Communication* (Urbana: University of Illinois Press, 1954).
3. D. Lerner, *The Passing of Traditional Society* (NY: The Free Press 1964).
4. E. McAnany (ed.), *Communications in the Rural Third World: The Role of Information in Development* (NY: Praeger, 1980).
5. W. Schramm, *Mass Media and National Development* (Stanford: Stanford University Press, 1964).
6. D. McClelland, *The Achieving Society* (NY: Van Notrand, 1961).
7. R.C. Benge, *Communication and Identity* (London: Bingley, 1972).
8. T. Schwartz, *The Responsive Chord* (Garden City, NY: Anchor Books, 1973).

CHAPTER 7

1. G. Miller, *The Psychology of Communication: Seven Essays* (NY: Basic Books, 1967).
2. O. Klapp, *Opening and Closing* (NY: Oxford University Press, 1978), ch. 4.
3. J.G. March and H.A. Simon, *Organizations* (NY: Wiley, 1958), ch. 6.
4. March and Simon, ch. 7.
5. E. Rogers and L. Kincaid, *Communication Networks* (NY: Free Press, 1981).

CHAPTER 8

1. G. Bateson, "Information and Codification," in J. Ruesch and G. Bateson, *Communication: The Social Matrix of Psychiatry* (NY: Norton, 1951), p. 179.
2. Bateson, personal communication, June, 1974.
3. P. Watzlawick and others, *Pragmatics of Human Communication* (NY: Norton, 1967), ch. 2.
4. B. Bernstein, "Elaborated and Restricted Codes: Their Social Origins and Some Consequences," in *Communication and Culture,* ed. A.G. Smith (NY: Holt, Rinehart and Winston, 1966), pp. 427-41.

CHAPTER 9

1. R. Jakobson, "Verbal Communication," *Scientific American*, Sept. (1972), pp. 73-80.
2. J.H. Greenberg, ed., *Universals of Language* (Cambridge: MIT Press, 1963).
3. J. Searle, "What is a Speech Act?" in *Language and Social Context*, ed. P.P. Giglioli (Baltimore: Penguin, 1972), pp. 136-54.
4. D. Hymes, *Foundations in Sociolinguistics: An Ethnographic Approach* (Philadelphia: University of Pennsylvania Press, 1974), p. 18.
5. S. Langer, *Philosophy in a New Key* (Cambridge: Harvard University Press, 1942), pp. 79-102.

CHAPTER 10

1. G. Bateson, *Steps to an Ecology of Mind* (NY: Ballantine, 1972), p. 189.
2. E. Goffman, *Frame Analysis: An Essay on the Organization of Experience* (Cambridge: Harvard University Press, 1974), pp. 124-155.
3. Goffman, p. 137.
4. G. Tuchman, *Making News* (NY: The Free Press, 1978), p. 193.
5. Tuchman, ch. 9.
6. K. Burke, "Dramatism," in *Communication: Concepts and Perspectives*, ed. L. Thayer (Washington: Spartan Books, 1967), p. 359.
7. *Ibid.*

CHAPTER 11

1. H.D. Duncan, "Communication and Social Order, in F.W. Matson and A. Montagu, ed., *The Human Dialogue* (NY: The Free Press, 1967), pp. 383-96.
2. M. Edelman, *The Symbolic Uses of Politics* (Urbana: University of Illinois Press, 1964). p. 6.
3. *Ibid.*, ch. 1.
4. M. Edelman, *Politics as Symbolic Action* (NY: Academic Press, 1971), ch. 6.
5. M. Edelman, *Political Language: Words that Succeed and Policies that Fail* (NY: Academic Press, 1977).
6. R. Barthes, *Elements of Semiology* (London: Cape, 1967), ch. 4; Barthes, *System de la mode* (Paris: Editions du Seuil, 1967).
7. *Wall Street Journal*, 9 March, 1978.
8. E. Leach, *Culture and Communication* (Cambridge: Cambridge University Press, 1976).

CHAPTER 12

1. L.S. Vygotsky, *Mind in Society: The Development of Higher Psychological Processes* (Cambridge: Harvard Univ. Press, 1978).
2. H. Furth, *Thinking Without Language* (NY: The Free Press, 1966).
3. *Ibid.*, p. 154.
4. E.A. Tinbergen and N. Tinbergen, *Early Childhood Autism: An Ethological approach* (Berlin: Paul Parey, 1972).
5. *Ibid.*
6. W. Percy, *The Message in the Bottle – How Queer Man Is, How Queer Language Is, and What One Has To Do With the Other* (NY: Farrar, Straus & Giroux, 1975), ch. 1.
7. H. Keller, *The Story of My Life* (NY: Doubleday, 1954), quoted in Percy, pp. 34-5.

PART FOUR

1. C. Geertz, *The Interpretation of Cultures* (NY: Basic Books, 1973), p. 24.
2. F. de Saussure, *Course in General Linguistics* (NY: McGraw Hill, 1966).

CHAPTER 13

1. W.C. Gogel, "The Adjacency Principle in Visual Perception," *Scientific American*, 238 (1978), pp. 126-37.
2. Quoted in J. O'Hara, *Appointment in Samarra* (NY: Grosset & Dunlap, 1934).
3. R.L. Birdwhistell, "Some Body Motion Elements Accompanying Spoken American English," in *Communication*, ed. L. Thayer (Wash: Spartan Books, 1967).
4. E. Goffman, *Asylums* (Garden City, NY: Anchor, 1961); R. Birdwhistell, *Kinesics and Context* (Piladelphia: University of Pennsylvania Press, 1970).
5. E.T. Hall, "Silent Assumptions in Social Communication," in *The Human Dialogue*, ed. F.W. Matson and A. Montagu (NY: Free Press, 1967), pp. 491-505.
6. E.T. Hall, *The Silent Language* (NY: Doubleday, 1959), ch. 1.
7. E.H. Gombrich, "The Visual Image," *Scientific American*, September (1972), pp. 82-96.
8. *Ibid.*, p. 89.
9. E.H. Gombrich, *Art and Illusion; A Study in the Psychology of Pictorial Representation* (NY: Pantheon Books, 1969), Part One.
10. B.L. Whorf, "The Name of the Situation as Affecting Behavior," in *Social Psychology through Symbolic Interaction*, ed. G. Stone and H. Farbermann (Toronto: Xerox College Publishing, 1970).
11. J. Berger, *Ways of Seeing* (London: BBC, 1972).

CHAPTER 14

1. P. Watzlawick, and others, *Change: Principles of Problem Formation and Problem Solution* (NY: Norton, 1974), p. 95.
2. M. McLuhan, *Understanding Media: The Extensions of Man* (NY: Signet Books, 1964); D.F. Theall, *The Medium is the Rear-View Mirror* (Montreal: McGill-Queen's Press, 1971).
3. H.A. Innis, *Empire and Communication* (Oxford: Clarendon, 1950); *The Bias of Communication* (Toronto: University of Toronto Press, 1951).
4. W. Kuhns, *The Post-Industrial Prophets: Interpretation of Technology* (NY: Weybright and Talley, 1971); J. Carey, "Canadian Communication Theory: Extensions and Interpretations of Harold Innis," in *Studies in Canadian Communications,* ed. G.J. Robinson and D.F. Theall (Montreal: McGill Programme in Communications, 1975), pp. 27-59.
5. *Ibid.*
6. J. Goody, *Communication and Evolution* (Cambridge: Cambridge University Press, 1977).
7. G. Bateson, *Mind and Nature* (NY: Dutton, 1979).

CHAPTER 15

1. J. Piaget, *Psychology and Epistemology* (NY: Grossman, 1971).
2. A. Tversky and D. Kahneman, "Judgment under Uncertainty: Heuristics and Bias," *Science,* 185 (1974), pp. 1124-1131.
3. *Ibid.,* p. 1126.
4. H. Terrace, *Nim: A Chimpanzee Who Learned Sign Language* (NY: Knopf, 1980).
5. R.L. Birdwhistell, *Microcultural Incidents in Ten Zoos* (Pennsylvania State University, 1971).
6. Langer, *Philosophy in a New Key* (Cambridge: Harvard Univ. Press, 1942), p. 15.
7. Glasgow University Media Group, *Bad News* (London: Routledge Kegan Paul, 1980).
8. U. Eco, "Can Television Teach?" Schools Television Conference, London, June, 1978, unpublished text.
9. E.J. Epstein, *News From Nowhere* (NY: Random House, 1973), p. 5.
10. D.J. Boorstin, *The Image – A Guide to Pseudo-Events in America* (NY: Atheneum, 1971).
11. R. Smith, "Mythic Elements in TV News," *Journal of Communication* Vol. 29, No. 1 (1979), pp. 75-82.
12. F. Friendly, *Due to Circumstances Beyond Our Control* (NY: Vintage, 1967).
13. H. Böll, *the Lost Honor of Katerina Blum* (NY: McGraw-Hill, 1975).

CHAPTER 16

1. J. Dewey, *The Public and Its Problems* (Chicago: Swallow Press, 1927).
2. R.E. Park, *Society: Collective Behavior, News and Opinion, Sociology and Modern Society* (Glencoe: The Free Press, 1955).
3. P. Lazarsfeld and H. Menzel, in *The Science of Human Communication*, ed. W. Schramm (NY: Basic Books, 1963), p. 96.
4. Klapper, *The Effects of Mass Communication* (NY: The Free Press, 1960).
5. A. Gouldner, *The Dialectic of Ideology and Technology* (NY: Seabury, 1976), ch. 4.
6. R. Sennett, *The Fall of Public Man* (NY: Knopf, 1974), part one.
7. J. Habermas, "The Public Sphere," *New German Critique*, Fall (1974), pp. 49-55.
8. Habermas, "Vorbereitende Bemerrkungen zu einer Theorie der kommunikativen Kompetenz," in J. Habermas and N. Luhmann, *Theorie der Gesellschaft oder Sozialtechnologie* (Frankfurt: Suhrkamp, 1971).
9. M. Horkheimer and T. Adorno, *Dialectic of Enlightenment* (NY: Herder and Herder, 1972).
10. L. Lowenthal, *Literature, Popular Culture and Society* (NY: Prentice Hall, 1961), ch. 4.
11. T. Adorno, "The Stars Down to Earth: The Los Angeles Times Astrology Column," *Telos*, 19 (1974), pp. 13-90.
12. C. Mueller, *Politics of Communication* (NY: Oxford, 1973).
13. *Ibid.*, p. 32.
14. *Ibid.*, pp. 100-101.

CHAPTER 17

1. H. Innis, *The Bias of Communication* (Toronto: U. of Toronto Pr., 1951), p. 82.
2. W. Melody and others, *Culture, Communication and Dependency: The Tradition of H.A. Innis* (Norwood, NJ: Ablex, 1981).
3. International Commission for the Study of Communication Problems (The MacBride Commission), *Many Voices, One World* (London: Kogan Page, 1980).
4. A. Mattelart, "Introduction: For a Class Analysis of Communication," in *Communication and Class Struggle*, ed. A. Mattelart and S. Siegelaub (NY: International General, 1979), pp. 23-70.
5. J. Tunstall, *The Media are American: Anglo-American Media in the World* (London: Constable, 1977); T.H. Gubach, *The International Film Industry: Western Europe and America since 1945* (Bloomington: Indiana University Press, 1969).
6. H. Schiller, *Communication and Cultural Domination* (White Plains: International Arts and Science Press, 1976).
7. E. Rogers, and L. Kincaid. *Communication Networks.* New York: The Free Press, 1981.

8. E. McAnany, ed., *Communications in the Rural Third World* (NY: Praeger, 1980).
9. E. Rogers, ed., Issue on Communication and Development: Critical Perspectives, *Communication Research*, Vol. 3, No. 2 (1976).
10. H. Felstehausen, "Conceptual Limits of Development Communications Theory," *Sociologia Ruralis*, Vol. 3, No. 1 (1973), pp. 39-53.
11. *Ibid.*, p. 40.
12. D. Hymes, "On the Origins and Foundations of Inequality Among Speakers," *Daedalus*, Vol. 102, No. 3 (1973), pp. 59-86.
13. *Ibid.*
14. *Ibid.*
15. *Ibid.*

CHAPTER 18

1. R. Williams, *Communication* (Baltimore: Penguin, 1962), p. 12.
2. R. Williams, *Television: Technology and Cultural Form* (London: Fontana, 1974), pp. 33-4.
3. Williams, 1962, p. 133.
4. R. Williams, *Marxism and Literature* (Oxford: Oxford University Press, 1977), ch. 6.
5. R. Williams, *The Country and the City* (NY: Oxford University Press, 1973).
6. Williams, 1977, p. 113.
7. *Ibid.*, chs. 8 and 9.
8. C. Geertz, *The Interpretation of Cultures* (NY: Basic Books, 1973), ch. 8.
9. *Ibid.*, p. 219.
10. J. Carey, "Communication and Culture," *Communication Research*, Vol. 2, No. 2 (1975), pp. 173-91.
11. *Ibid.*, p. 190.

CHAPTER 19

1. P.L. Berger and T. Luckmann, *The Social Construction of Reality* (Garden City, N.Y.: Anchor Books, 1966), ch. 2.
2. *Ibid.*, p. 108.
3. B. Holzner, *Reality Construction in Society* (Cambridge, Mass.: Schenkman, 1972), ch. 4.
4. G. Suttles, *The Social Construction of Community* (Chicago: University of Chicago Press, 1972), pp. 47-53.
5. T. Kuhn, *The Structure of Scientific Revolution* (Chicago: University of Chicago Press, 1970).

CHAPTER 20

1. E. Rogers, "Communication and Development: The Passing of the Dominant Paradigm," *Communication Research,* Vol. 3, No. 2 (1976), pp. 213-40.
2. J. Halloran, *Mass Media and Society* (Leicester: Leicester University Press, 1974).
3. *Ibid.,* p. 10.
4. A. Briggs, "Broadcasting and Social Change: Relationships under Review," in *Symposium on the Cultural Role of Broadcasting, Summary Report* (Tokyo: Hoso-Bunka Foundation, 1978), pp. 70-78.
5. D. Cater, "The Future of Communications Policy," in *Symposium on the Cultural Role of Broadcasting,* pp. 124-30.
6. L. Beltran, "Communication Research in Latin America: The Blindfolded Inquiry?" in *Internationale Wissenschaftliche Konferenz,* der Anteil der Massenmedien bei der Herausbildung des Bewusstseins in der sich wandelnden welt (Leipzig: Karl-Marx Universitat, 1974), pp. 370-93.
7. *New York Times,* "Text of UNESCO Declaration on News Organizations," 23 November, 1978, p. A 12.

CHAPTER 21

1. C. Lindblom, *The Intelligence of Democracy* (NY: The Free Press, 1965), p. 3.
2. J. Habermas, "A Review of Gadamer's *Truth and Method,*" in *Understanding and Social Inquiry,* ed. F. Dallmayr and T. McCarthy (Notre Dame: Notre Dame University Press, 1977), p. 353.

Index